Mary,
Mother of the Church

Mary, Mother of the Church

by

Rev. Francis J. Ripley

What recent Popes have said about the Blessed Mother's role in the Church.

TAN Books
Gastonia, North Carolina

Imprimatur: Michael Ward
Vicar General
Glasgow, Scotland
July 16, 1969

This edition originally published in England by Gracewing.

Retypeset and published in 2014 by TAN Books.

Cover image: The Virgin and Child Enthroned among Angels and Saints; Benozzo Gozzoli; 1461.

ISBN: 978-0-89555-094-1

Printed in India.
TAN Books
Gastonia, North Carolina
www.TANBooks.com
2012

FOREWORD

"In honor of the Blessed Virgin and for our comfort, We proclaim Mary Most Holy to be the Mother of the Church . . . We decree also that the whole Christian people should make use of this attractive title to increase the honor of the Mother of God in the prayers that they offer." So said Pope Paul VI to all the Catholic Bishops of the world as he closed the third session of the Second Vatican Council on November 21, 1964.

During that session, the Council approved the Dogmatic Constitution on the Church, of which the eighth chapter is devoted to Our Lady. Pope Paul called it the very headstone of the Constitution, "a matchless hymn in praise of the Virgin Mother of God." The Council's decision, under the guidance of Mary's Spouse, the Holy Spirit, to make the chapter on the Blessed Virgin part of the document on the Church, is immensely important. For too long devotion to Mary had been separated from the main stream of devotion to the Church; some had looked upon it as an extra, almost as a condiment to integral Catholicism. The Council ended all that by taking the tremendous accumulation of devotion to Mary during twenty centuries and putting it exactly where it belongs—in the setting of the Church.

The pages which follow contain some of the more important pronouncements of modern Popes about Mary's place in God's plan for our salvation and sanctification. When we read them prayerfully we see how and why they were so providential in preparing the way for the mighty Chapter 8. Not all are of equal importance, of course, but together they form a fair picture of the thought of the Vicars of Christ in the years before the Council. They show what the Council took and placed fairly and squarely in the context of the Church's definition of herself. They enable us to see why, as he went to Fatima on May 13, 1967, Pope Paul VI wrote to the bishops of the world begging them to arouse their people to "an ever more fervid and more fruitful Marian piety" so that every member of Christ would make his own the prayer of St. Anselm, Doctor of the Church and Archbishop of Canterbury: "O Glorious Lady, grant that through you we may deserve to ascend to Jesus, your Son, who through you deigned to descend among us."

FRANCIS J. RIPLEY.

CONTENTS

OUR LADY, MEDIATRIX OF ALL GRACES

What the Popes have said

MARY IS THE UNIVERSAL MEDIATRIX

1. "The zeal and love of the Blessed Virgin Mary have such influence in obtaining God's help for us that, just as through her, God came down to earth, so through her, man mounts up to heaven. But just as man's iniquity often calls down God's indignation, God's Mother is the rainbow of the eternal covenant for mankind's salvation. For, while the prayers of those in heaven have certainly some claim on the watchful eye of God, Mary's prayers place their assurance on the right of a mother. For that reason, when she approaches the throne of her Divine Son, she begs as advocate, she prays as handmaid, but she commands as mother." (Pius X: Apostolic Constitution, Tanto studio, February 19, 1905.)

Mary's Universal Mediation unanimously proclaimed by tradition

2. "Mary is this glorious intermediary . . . The plan of this most loving mercy, realized by God in Mary and

confirmed by the testament of Christ, was understood with the utmost joy by the holy Apostles and the earliest believers. It was the belief and teaching of the venerable Fathers of the Church. Christians of every generation received it with one mind." (Leo XIII: Encyclical, *Octobri mense*, September 22, 1891.)

3. "The scene of Jesus' birth is complete through Mary's presence. The faith of her believers and her children's love consider her not only God's mother, but also the mediatrix with God." (Benedict XV: Christmas Allocution, December 24, 1915.)

She is the Mediatrix of Mediators

4. "We think God has so disposed matters to remind the faithful that we must never forget Mary even when the miracle seems to be attributed to the intercession or the mediation of one who has been beatified or canonised . . . On the one hand Our Lord shows us that even on this earth, which is entrusted to His blessed Mother's care, He can work miracles through the intercession of one of His servants; on the other hand, He reminds us that even in such cases it is necessary to postulate the intercession of her whom the Holy Father greeted as *Mediatrix Mediatorum omnium.*" (Discourse of the Bishop of Orleans to pilgrims present at the approval of the miracles for the canonisation of Joan of Arc, April 6, 1919.)

5. "This grace (i.e. health regained) we attribute to the special intercession of the Virgin of Lisieux, St.

Teresa of the Child Jesus. But at the same time we know that every blessing that comes to us from Almighty God comes through Our Lady's hands." (Pius XI: Encyclical, *Ingravescentibus malis*, September 29, 1937.)

She is Mediatrix between Christ and the Church

6. "Set up between Christ and His Church, Mary, ever lovable and full of grace, has always delivered the Christian people from their greatest calamities, ever rescued them from ruin." (Pius IX: Encyclical, *Ubi primum*, February 2, 1849.)

Mary is Mediatrix to the Mediator

7. "Now that the anniversary of manifold and exceedingly great favors obtained by a Christian people through the devotion of the Rosary is at hand, We desire that the same devotion should be offered by the whole Catholic world with the greatest earnestness to the Blessed Virgin, in order that by her intercession her divine Son may be appeased and moved to compassion towards us in the miseries which afflict us." (Leo XIII: Encyclical, *Supremi Apostolatus*, September 1, 1883.)

8. "As the Angelic Doctor teaches: 'There is no reason why certain others should not be called in a certain way mediators between God and man, that is to say insofar as they cooperate by predisposing and ministering in the union of man with God.' Such are the Angels and Saints, the prophets and priests of both Testaments, but especially has the Blessed Virgin a claim to

the glory of this title. For no single individual can even be imagined who has ever contributed or ever will contribute so much towards reconciling man with God. To mankind heading for eternal ruin, she offered a Saviour when she received the announcement of the mystery brought to this earth by the Angel, and in giving her consent gave it in the name of the whole human race. She it is from whom Jesus is born; therefore she is truly His Mother and for this reason a worthy and acceptable 'Mediatrix to the Mediator.'" (Leo XIII: Encyclical, *Fidentem Piumque*, September 20, 1896.)

9. "From this community of will and suffering between Christ and Mary she merited to become most worthily the reparatrix of the lost world and dispensatrix of all the gifts that Our Saviour bought for us by His death and by His blood . . . By this union in sorrow and suffering, as We have said, which existed between the Mother and the Son, it has been allowed to the august Virgin to be the most powerful Mediatrix and advocate of the whole world with her divine Son." (St. Pius X: Encyclical, *Ad diem illum*, February 2, 1904.)

10. "May the most gracious Mother of God, who gave us Jesus as Redeemer, who reared Him, and at the foot of the Cross offered Him as Victim, who by her mysterious union with Christ and by her matchless grace rightly merits the name Reparatrix, deign to smile upon our wishes and our undertakings, trusting in her intercession with Christ Our Lord, who although He is the only Mediator between God and man, still wished

to make His mother the advocate for sinners and the dispenser and Mediatrix of His grace." (Pius XI: Encyclical, *Miserentissimus Redemptor*, May 8, 1928.)

11. "In fact, the august Virgin, conceived without original sin, was chosen to be the Mother of Christ in order to be associated with Him in the redemption of mankind. For that reason she was adorned with such abundant grace and such great power in her Son's sight that neither human nor angelic nature can ever acquire a like grace or power." (Pius XI: Letter, *Auspicatus Profecto*, to Cardinal Binet, January 28, 1933.)

All is accomplished through the intercession of Mary

12. "The foundation of all our confidence . . . is found in the Blessed Virgin Mary. God has committed to her the treasury of all good things, in order that everyone may know that through her are obtained every hope, every grace, and all salvation. For this is His will, that we obtain everything through Mary." (Pius IX: Encyclical, *Ubi primum*, February 2, 1849.)

13. "O Virgin most holy, none abounds in the knowledge of God except through thee; none, O Mother of God, obtains salvation except through thee, none receives a gift from the throne of mercy except through thee." (Leo XIII: Encyclical, *Adiutricem populi*, September 5, 1895.)

14. "God alone gives grace according to the measure which in His infinite wisdom He foresees. But,

although that grace comes from God, it is given through Mary, our Advocate and Mediatrix, since motherly affection on the one hand finds response in childlike devotion on the other." (Pius XI: Address to Pilgrims, August 15, 1933.)

15. "We beseech God through the mediation of the Blessed Virgin, so acceptable to Him, since, to use St. Bernard's words: 'Such is the will of God who has wished that we should have all things through Mary.'" (Pius XI: Encyclical, *Ingravescentibus malis*, September 29, 1937.)

16. "Since, as St. Bernard declares, 'It is the will of God that we obtain all favors through Mary,' let everyone hasten to have recourse to Mary . . . So powerful indeed is the Blessed Virgin with God and His only begotten Son that, as Dante writes, anyone who desires His help and fails to have recourse to Mary is like one trying to fly without wings." (Pius XII: Letter, *Superiore anno*, to Cardinal Maglione, April 15, 1940.)

17. "May she, who has given us Jesus, obtain for us that all those who have wandered from the path of truth may immediately return to Him moved by salutary contrition. May she obtain for us—she is our kindest mother, who has always shown herself in the face of every danger our powerful helper and channel of grace—may she obtain for us, we say, that even in the midst of the gravest need surrounding us, a just solution may be found . . ." (Pius XII: Encyclical, *Auspicia quaedam*, May 1, 1948.)

By means of Mary, Christians receive divine life

18. "By God's will, the most Blessed Virgin Mary was inseparably joined with Christ in accomplishing the work of man's redemption, so that our salvation flows from the love of Jesus Christ and His sufferings intimately united with the love and sorrows of His mother." (Pius XII: Encyclical, *Haurietis aquas*, May 15, 1956.)

We go to Jesus through Mary

19. "God's eternal Son, about to take upon Himself our nature for the saving and ennobling of man, and about to consummate thus a mystical union between Himself and all mankind, did not accomplish His design without obtaining the free consent of her who was to become His mother. She was the representative of all mankind, according to the illustrious and learned opinion of St. Thomas, who says that 'in the annunciation was awaited the consent of the virgin who represented humanity.' With equal truth it may be said that of the great treasury of all graces given to us by Our Lord—for grace and truth came by Jesus Christ—nothing comes to us except through Mary's mediation, for such is God's Will. Thus, as no man goes to the Father but by the Son, so no one goes to Christ except through His mother." (Leo XIII Encyclical, *Octobri mense*, September 22, 1891.)

20. "If it is impossible to separate what God has united, it is also certain that you cannot find Jesus

except with Mary and through Mary." (St. Pius X: Allocution to the Franciscans, November 12, 1910.)

21. "Since all the graces which God deigns to bestow in pity upon men are dispensed through the Most Holy Virgin, we urge that . . . the trusting petitions of her most afflicted children be directed to the august Mother of God . . . It is our fervent desire that mankind turn to the Sacred Heart of Jesus, the throne of grace, and that recourse to this throne be made through Mary." (Benedict XV: Letter to Cardinal Gasparri, April 27, 1915.)

22. "You see in him (St. Louis Marie de Montfort) . . . the guide who leads you to Mary and through Mary to Jesus." (Pius XII: Allocution at the Canonisation of St. Louis Marie de Montfort, July 21, 1947.)

23. "Every day, as the Church herself recommends, priests will recite the Holy Rosary, which, by proposing for our meditation the mysteries of the Redeemer, leads us to Jesus through Mary." (Pius XII: Exhortation, *Menti nostri*, September 23, 1950.)

24. "Active members of Catholic Action will look up to Mary, who is the surest means of leading souls to Jesus." (Pius XII: Radio message to the Lebanese Marian Congress, October 23, 1950.)

25 "Dearest Mother, our delight and our hope, lead us to Jesus, the blessed fruit of thy womb, so that if we have not enjoyed the sweetness of a mother here below, we may hereafter, in everlasting life, enjoy thy

motherly love and thy presence, together with that of thy divine Son." (Pius XII: Prayer, *Salve, O Vergine*, August 28, 1956.)

Mary is always well accepted by her Son

26. "Just as all things created acknowledge and obey God's Will, so may it be stated that Mary's Son ever attends most favorably to His Mother's petitions and especially so now that she enjoys eternal happiness in heaven." (Pius XII: Letter to Cardinal Maglione, April 15, 1942.)

Mary's charge is not contrary to Christ's mediation

27. "Who could think or say that the confidence so strongly felt in the Blessed Virgin's patronage is excessive. Undoubtedly the name and attributes of the absolute Mediator belong to no other than Christ, for being one person and yet both Man and God, He restored the human race to the favor of the heavenly Father. 'Only one mediator between God and men, Jesus Christ, who is a man like them and gave Himself as a ransom for them all' (1 Tim. 2, 5-6) and yet, as the Angelical Doctor teaches: 'There is no reason why certain others should not be called in a certain way mediators between God and man . . . especially has the Blessed Virgin a claim to the glory of this title.'" (Leo XIII: Encyclical, *Fidentum Piumque*, September 20, 1896.)

The Office of Our Lady as Mediatrix appears especially in the Rosary

28. "The recourse we have to Mary in prayer follows upon the office she continuously fills by the side of the throne of God as Mediatrix of divine grace, being by worthiness and by merit more acceptable to Him, and for that reason surpassing in power all the angels and saints in heaven. Now, this merciful office of hers appears perhaps in no other form of prayer as manifestly as it does in the Rosary. For in the Rosary the part that Mary took as our Co-Redemptrix is set before us." (Leo XIII: Encyclical, *Jucunda semper*, September 8, 1894.)

29. "As the various mysteries present themselves one after another in the formula of the Rosary, for the meditation and contemplation of men's minds, they also make clear what we owe to Mary for our reconciliation and salvation. No one can fail to be sweetly affected when he considers who appeared in Elizabeth's home as the minister of the divine gifts, who presented her Son to the shepherds, the kings and Simeon. One must remember, too, that Christ's blood shed for our sake and those members in which He offers to His Father the wounds He received as the price of our freedom are no other than the flesh and blood of the virgin. The flesh of Jesus is the flesh of Mary, and however much it was exalted in the glory of His Resurrection, still the nature of His flesh which He took from Mary remained and still remains the same."

(Leo XIII: Encyclical, *Fidentum Piumque*, September 20,1896.)

GOD WILLED OUR LADY'S MEDIATION

30. "May God, who in His most merciful providence gave us this mediatrix and decreed that all good should come to us by the hands of Mary, receive propitiously our common prayer and fulfil our common hopes." (Leo XIII: Encyclical, *Jucunda semper*, September 8, 1894.)

31. "It is by means of her, of her who is the 'mirror of justice' and the 'seat of wisdom,' that Almighty God ordained that we should receive everything. When the wise men went to Bethlehem to adore Jesus they found on entering into the house the Child with Mary His mother." (St. Pius X: Allocution to the Franciscans, November 12, 1910.)

32. "With Our Lord may she be blessed whom He constituted Mother of Mercy, Queen and Our Most Loving Advocate, Mediatrix of His Graces, Dispenser of His Treasures." (Pius XII: Radio Message to Fatima on May 13, 1946.)

33. "Among the saints of heaven, the Virgin Mary, Mother of God, is the recipient of a more exalted worship. Because of the office she received from God, her life is closely linked with Christ's mysteries . . . She became our Mother when the divine Redeemer was

consummating the sacrifice of Himself; therefore, by this title, also, we are her children. She teaches us all the virtues; she gives us her Son, and with Him all the help we need, for God has willed that we should have everything through Mary." (Pius XII: Encyclical, *Mediator Dei*, November 20, 1947.)

34. "It is highly fitting that after due homage has been paid to the Most Sacred Heart of Jesus, Christian people who have obtained divine life from Christ through Mary manifest similar piety and love of their grateful souls for the most loving heart of our heavenly Mother." (Pius XII: Encyclical, *Haurietis aquas*, May 15, 1956.)

See also quotations 2, 19 and 21 above.

God willed that we should receive Jesus from Mary

35. "God could have given us the Redeemer of the human race and the Founder of the Faith in another way than through the Virgin, but since divine Providence has been pleased that we should have the Man-God through Mary, who conceived Him by the Holy Ghost and bore Him in her womb, it only remains for us to receive Christ through the hands of Mary." (St. Pius X: Encyclical, *Ad diem illum*, February 2, 1904.)

36. "Devotion to Mary will make possible in you a better understanding of Christ and a more intense union with His mysteries. You will receive Christ from His mother's arms and she will allow you to love Him

and imitate Him." (Pius XII: Allocution to Women of Catholic Action, September 29, 1957.)

God willed that Mary should give Christ to the world

37. "The Most Holy Virgin was a providential instrument, chosen in the designs of our heavenly Father, to give and present His incomparable Son to the world, to be the Mother and Queen of the Apostles who were to spread His doctrine all over the world, ever to check heresies and also to intervene always in a wonderful manner wherever necessary to introduce, strengthen and defend the Holy Catholic Faith. In this connection, one of her great servants, St. Cyril of Alexandria, writes as follows: 'Through her the holy Cross is known and adored all over the world; through her every creature imprisoned by the bonds of idolatrous errors comes to the knowledge of truth; through her the Apostles preached salvation to the nations.'" (Pius XII: Radio message to the Marian Congress in Mexico, October 12, 1945.)

38. "God has committed to the Blessed Virgin Mary the treasury of all good things in order that everyone may know that through her are obtained every hope, every grace and all salvation." (Pius IX: Encyclical, *Ubi primum*, February 2, 1894.)

39. "All our hope do we repose in the Most Blessed Virgin, in the all-fair and immaculate one who has crushed the most cruel serpent's poisonous head and

brought salvation to the world . . . In her who, with her only begotten Son, is the most powerful mediatrix and conciliatrix in the whole world . . . In her who has destroyed all heresies and snatched the faithful people and nations from all kinds of direst calamities . . . We are firm in our confidence that she will obtain pardon for the sinner, health for the sick, strength of heart for the weak, consolation for the afflicted, help for those in danger; that she will remove spiritual blindness from all who are in error, so that they may return to the path of truth and justice, and there may be one flock and one shepherd." (Pius IX: Apostolic Constitution, *Ineffabilis Deus*, December 8, 1854.)

40. "Let all the children of the Catholic Church . . . continue to venerate, invoke and pray to the Most Blessed Virgin Mary . . . Under her guidance, under her patronage, under her kindness and protection, nothing is to be feared, nothing is hopeless, because, while bearing towards us a truly motherly affection and having in her care the work of our salvation, she is solicitous about the whole human race . . . She presents our petitions in a most efficacious manner. What she asks she obtains. Her pleas can never be unheard." (Pius IX: Apostolic Constitution, *Ineffabilis Deus*, December 8, 1854.)

41. "It is a great thing in any saint to have grace sufficient for the salvation of many souls, but to have enough to suffice for the salvation of everybody in the world is the greatest of all, and that is found in Christ

and in the Blessed Virgin." (Leo XIII: Encyclical, *Magnae Dei Matris*, September 8, 1892.)

42. "Every time we say (the words of the Hail Mary) we recall the memory of her exalted dignity and of the redemption of the human race which God began through her. We likewise bring to mind the divine and everlasting bond which links her with the joys and sorrows, the humiliations and triumphs of Christ in directing and helping mankind to eternal life . . . Because Mary was chosen to be the Mother of Christ, Our Lord and Our Brother, the unique prerogative was given her above all other mothers to show her mercy to us and to pour it out upon us." (Leo XIII: Encyclical, *Magnae Dei Matris*, September 8, 1892.)

43. "O Holy Mother of God; to thee we lift our prayers for thou, powerful and merciful, art the Mediatrix of our salvation." (Leo XIII: Encyclical, *Jucunda semper*, September 8, 1894.)

44. "None, O Mother of God, obtains salvation except through thee, none receives a gift from the throne of mercy except through thee." (Leo XIII: *Adiutricem populi*, September 5, 1895.)

45. "May the most powerful Virgin Mary, who at one time by her charity co-operated in the birth of the faithful in the Church, be still the instrument and guardian of our salvation." (Leo XIII: Apostolic Letter, *Parta humano generi*, September 8, 1901.)

46. See quotation No. 9.

47. "Mary in the work of redemption was by God's will joined with Jesus Christ, the cause of salvation, in much the same way as Eve was joined with Adam, the cause of death. Hence it can be said that the work of our salvation was brought about by a restoration in which the human race, just as it was doomed to death by a virgin, was saved by a virgin. Moreover, she was chosen to be the Mother of Christ in order to have part with Him in the redemption of the human race." (Pius XII: Encyclical, *Ad coeli Reginam*, October 11, 1954.)

Mary is Mediatrix to repair our fall

48. "They (the Fathers) also declared that the most glorious Virgin was Reparatrix of the first parents, the giver of life to posterity; that she was chosen before the ages, prepared for Himself by the Most High, foretold by God when He said to the serpent, 'I will put enmities between thee and the woman'—unmistakable evidence that she has crushed the serpent's poisonous head." (Pius IX: Apost. Coast., *Ineffabilis Deus*, December 8, 1854.)

49. "When in the beginning of the human race, the parents of mankind fell into sin, involving their descendants in the same ruin, Mary was set up as the pledge of the restoration of peace and salvation." (Leo XIII: Encyclical, *Augustissimae*, September 12, 1897.)

Mary leads us to Jesus

50. "The unexampled part which the Virgin most

admirably played and still plays in the progress, the battles and the triumph of the Catholic Faith, makes it clear what God has planned for her to do . . . Remembering that her only-begotten Son prayed so earnestly to His heavenly Father for the closest union among the nations whom He has called by the one baptism to the one inheritance of salvation bought for an infinite price, will she not, for that reason, see to it that all in this marvellous light will strive as with one mind for unity? And will it not be her wish to employ her goodness and providence to console the Spouse of Christ, the Church, through her long sustained efforts in this enterprise, as well as to bring to full perfection the boon of unity among the members of the Christian family, which is the illustrious fruit of her motherhood?" (Leo XIII: Encyclical, *Adiutricem populi*, September 5, 1895.)

51. "Can anyone fail to see that there is no surer and more direct road than by Mary for uniting all mankind in Christ and obtaining through Him the perfect adoption of sons, that we may be holy and immaculate in the sight of God?" (St. Pius X: Encyclical, *Ad diem illum*, February 2, 1904.)

52. "When one reflects that with her alone did Jesus spend thirty years in that family union of Son and Mother, surely there is no doubt that through Mary the surest way of knowing Christ is opened to us . . . Nobody ever knew Christ so profoundly as she did, and nobody can ever be more competent as a guide

and teacher of the knowledge of Christ." (St. Pius X: Encyclical, *Ad diem illum*, February 2, 1904.)

53. "The Blessed Virgin is more powerful than all others as means of uniting mankind with Christ. In fact, if, as Christ said, 'Now this is eternal life; that they may know thee, the only true God and Jesus Christ whom thou has sent,' and, if through Mary we attain to the knowledge of Christ, through Mary we most easily obtain that life of which Christ is the source and origin." (St. Pius X: Encyclical, *Ad diem illum*, February 2, 1904.)

54. "One might say that Mary's only occupation was to take care of the Christian people . . . above all of attracting all souls to love and seek God." (St. Pius X: Letter to Cardinal Pignatelli, July 12, 1914.)

55. "Nothing must ever make us forget the reality and the knowledge that we are, all of us, sons of the same mother Mary, who lives in heaven, who is the bond of union for the Mystical Body of Christ, and who as the new Eve, and the new mother of the living, desires to lead all men to the truth and the grace of her divine Son." (Pius XII: Apostolic Constitution, *Munificemissimus Deus*, November 1, 1950.)

56. "Mary has no other desire but to lead men to Christ and to introduce them to the heart of the redemption. She continues to give to the Church the Son she brought into the world. If she loves to see her children assembled for a stirring manifestation of faith and love, it is to lead them together to the mysti-

cal bread, symbol of unity, of peace and of the eternal joy of heaven." (Pius XII: Radio message to the Belgian Marian Congress, September 5, 1954.)

Mary makes us sons by giving us a filial spirit

57. "Ask the Immaculate Virgin to obtain for you a childlike spirit towards God as she prayed in her *Magnificat*, her face turned toward the Almighty with gratitude and joy. May she teach you docility as she did at Cana when she advised the servants to do all that her divine Son might tell them. Last of all, may she obtain for you a far-reaching fraternal and apostolic charity, as she obtained it by her prayer in the midst of the first Christians gathered at the Cenacle." (Pius XII: Allocution to the Children of Mary, July 17, 1954.)

Mary offers us Divine Life

58. See quotation 53 above.

59. "Whenever we speak of Mary or speak to her, let us not forget that she is really our Mother, for through her we received divine life. She gave us Jesus Himself, the source of grace. Mary is a Mediatrix and Dispenser of Graces." (Pius XII: Radio message to the Italian Catholic Action, December 8, 1953.)

60. "Be like Mary, be with her the means of life to souls that are dying of hunger and cold, that, if stirred by your words and incited by your example, might return to their Father's house." (Pius XII: Radio message to the Italian Catholic Action, December 8, 1953.)

MARY IS THE MOTHER OF MERCY

61. "Mary is our Mother, the mother of pity and of grace, the mother of mercy, to whom Christ Our Lord in His dying breath on the Cross entrusted us, in order that, as He implores His heavenly Father for us, she may likewise entreat her Son on our behalf." (Pius VIII: Apostolic Constitution, *Praestantissimum sane*, March 3, 1830.)

62. "Do not cease to beg insistently this most beloved Mother of grace, Mary, to help and support by her powerful intercession with her Son our weakness, weighed down as We are by the very heavy solicitude for all the churches in such troubled times for Christianity." (Gregory XVI: Letter to the Archbishop of Prague, April 23, 1845.)

63. "Let them fly with utter confidence to this most sweet Mother of mercy and grace in all dangers, difficulties, needs, doubts and fears. Under her guidance, under her patronage, under her kindness and protection, nothing is to be feared, nothing is hopeless." (Pius IX Apostolic Constitution, *Ineffabilis Deus*, December 8, 1854.)

64. "Let us in all confidence choose as advocate before God the Immaculate and Most Holy Mother of God, the Virgin Mary. She has destroyed all the heresies of the world. She is our most loving Mother, all mild and merciful she shows herself within reach of every prayer; most kind, she takes to herself all our

needs with profound love and tender pity. In heaven as Queen at the right hand of her only Son, clothed in golden raiment and all manner of jewels, there is nothing she cannot obtain from Him." (Pius IX: Encyclical, *Quanta cura*, December 8, 1864.)

65. "How great are the goodness and mercy revealed in this design of God. What a boon to the frailty of man. We believe in the infinite goodness of the Most High and we rejoice in it, we believe also in His justice and we fear it. We adore the beloved Saviour who generously gave His blood and His life; but at the same time we dread the inexorable Judge. Thus do those whose actions have disturbed their consciences need an intercessor mighty in favor with God, merciful enough not to reject the cause of the desperate, merciful enough to lift up the afflicted and the broken in loving trust in the divine mercy. Mary is this glorious intermediary. She is the mighty Mother of God. But what is still sweeter, she is gentle, exquisite in tenderness, and of a limitless love and kindness. As such God gave her to us. Mother of His only begotten Son, He taught her all a mother's feelings that breathe pardon and love." (Leo XIII: Encyclical, *Octobri mense*, September 22, 1891.)

66. "Nothing is more natural, nothing more desirable, than to seek a refuge in the protection and the loyalty of her to whom we may confess our designs and our actions, and our repentance, our torments and our joys, our prayers and our desires—all our interests. All men, moreover, are full of the hope and confidence

that prayers which might be received with less favor from the lips of unworthy men, will be accepted by God when they are recommended to Him by the Most Holy Mother and will be favorably heard." (Leo XIII: Encyclical, *Octobri mense*, September 22, 1891.)

67. "When we have recourse to Mary in prayer we are having recourse to the Mother of mercy, so well disposed towards us that, whatever the necessity that presses upon us, especially in attaining eternal life, she is instantly at our side of her own accord, even though she has not been invoked." (Leo XIII: Encyclical, *Magnae Dei Matris*, September 8, 1892.)

68. "St. Dominic knew well that while on the one hand Mary is all powerful with her divine Son who grants all graces to mankind through her, on the other hand she is by nature so good and so merciful that inclined to aid spontaneously those who suffer, she is absolutely incapable of refusing her help to those who invoke her. The Church is in the habit of greeting the Virgin as *Mother of Grace* and *Mother of Mercy*, and so she has always shown herself, especially when we have recourse to her by means of the Holy Rosary." (Benedict XV: Encyclical, *Fausto appetente die*, June 29, 1921.)

69. "Mother most faithful and most merciful, who as Co-Redemptrix and partaker of thy dear Son's sorrows didst assist Him as He offered the sacrifice of our redemption on the altar of the Cross, preserve in us and increase each day, we beseech thee, the precious

fruits of our redemption and thy compassion." (Pius XI: Radio message to the Pilgrims at Lourdes, April 28, 1935.)

70. "If in her humility as handmaid of the Lord, all generations call her, and shall call her, blessed, the voice of our age also unites itself to the canticles of the past and future; in Mary it exalts a mother's heart, becoming sublime in the heavenly Child that she carries in her arms and presses to her breast. He is her heart's delight and the delight of the world; from His kiss springs up that fire of love which makes her Mother of Mercy and magnanimous clemency towards every child of Adam." (Pius XII: Allocution to Pilgrims from Genoa, April 21, 1940.)

71. "Since Mary is 'Mother of Mercy, our life, our sweetness and our hope,' let us cry to her, 'mourning and weeping in the vale of tears,' and place ourselves and all that is ours confidently under her patronage. She became our Mother when the divine Redeemer was consummating the sacrifice of Himself; hence, by this title also, we are her children." (Pius XII: *Mediator Dei*, November 20, 1947.)

72. "We nourish the great hope that the beloved Mother of God, crowned with new glory on earth, may contemplate with loving gaze, and bind to herself those who languish in spiritual apathy, or loathfully daily in the snares of vice, or who, having lost the straight way of truth, do not recognise that sublime dignity of hers with which the privilege of her bodily Assumption into

Heaven is strictly connected." (Pius XII: Allocution to the Consistory, October 30, 1950.)

73. "We trust that your merciful eyes may deign to gaze down upon our misery and anguish, upon our struggles and our weaknesses; that your countenance may smile upon our joys and our victories; that you may hear the voice of Jesus saying to you of each one of us, as He once said to you of His beloved disciple: 'Behold thy son,' and we who call upon you as our mother, we, like John, take you as the guide, strength and consolation of our mortal life." (Pius XII: Allocution to the faithful assembled in St. Peter's Square, November 1, 1950.)

Our Lady fulfils her office as Mediatrix with motherly generosity

74. "In our day, Mary, with the ever-merciful affection so characteristic of her motherly heart, wishes, through her efficacious prayer with God, to deliver her children from the sad and grief-laden troubles, from the tribulations, the anxiety, the difficulties and the punishments of God's anger, which afflict the world because of men's sins. Wishing to restrain and to dispel the violent hurricane of evils which are everywhere afflicting the Church, Mary desires to transform our sadness into joy." (Pius IX: Encyclical, *Ubi primum*, February 2, 1849.)

75. "We know that there is sure help in the motherly affection of the Blessed Virgin, and we are very certain

that we shall never place our trust in her in vain. If on innumerable occasions she has displayed her power in aid of the Christian world, why should we doubt that she will now renew the assistance of her power and favor if humble and constant prayers are offered on all sides to her? Nay, we rather believe that her intervention will be the more marvellous as she has permitted us to pray to her for so long a time with special appeals." (Leo XIII: Encyclical, *Quamquam pluries*, August 15, 1889.)

76. See quotation No. 65 above.

77. "While nature itself made the name of mother the sweetest of all names and has made motherhood the very model of tender and careful love, no tongue is eloquent enough to put in words what every devout soul feels, namely, how intense is the flame of affectionate and eager charity which glows in Mary, in her who is truly our Mother, not by nature but by the will of Christ." (Leo XII: Encyclical, *Magnae Dei Matris*, Sept. 8, 1892.)

78. "While the last world war was raging, while every kind of atrocity was committed on land, on sea and in the air, terrified men almost convinced themselves that no shred of goodness remained any longer in human hearts. Those who think like this have forgotten that motherly heart which beats with most tender love in union with the most sweet Heart of Jesus, her Child. The tenderness of the Immaculate Heart of Mary is in a certain sense infinite, with that infinity with which the Angelic Doctor (i.e. St. Thomas Aqui-

nas) said belonged to the Mother of God by reason of her consanguinity with God. The Mellifluous Doctor (i.e. St. Bernard) declared that the soul of the Most Blessed Virgin is full of the most ardent affection. And as in the midst of a world grown cold, there was need to rekindle the fire from heaven, we wished, on the Feast of the Immaculate Conception of the Blessed Virgin, in the year 1942, to consecrate all mankind forever to the Immaculate Heart of Mary." (Pius XII: Apostolic Letter, *Novissimo universarum*, May 1, 1947.)

79. "The restoration of a high moral tone to the life, work and love of the human family through the merits of Our Lord and Saviour was first and forever accomplished with the aid of a woman, ever humbly alert to the responsibilities of her motherly mission among the children of men." (Pius XII: Allocution to the Canadian Women's Press Club, July 2, 1955.)

Our Lady is most tender, compassionate and indulgent

80. "So that God may more eagerly hear our prayers and supplications, let us lift our eyes and hands to the Blessed Mother Mary, immaculate virgin. We could not find a more powerful protectoress or one more irresistible before God. She is for us the best of mothers, our safest confidante and in fact the very motive of our hope; she obtains all she asks for and her prayer is always heard." (Pius IX: Encyclical, *Exultavit cor Nostrum*, November 21, 1851.)

81. See quotation No. 66 above.

82. See quotations Nos. 41 and 67 above.

83. "Mary, without having herself experienced them, yet who knows our weakness and defects of our fallen nature, she who is the best and most devoted of mothers, how quickly and generously she will come to our aid! With what tenderness she will comfort us ! With what strength she will support us! Travelling the road which the divine Blood of Christ and Mary's tears have consecrated, we are certain to attain without trouble to a share in her blessed glory." (Leo XIII: Encyclical, *Magnae Dei Matris*, September 8, 1892.)

84. "(Our Rosaries) acquire yet another title of joy and acceptance in Mary's eyes. For every time we look once more with devotion and remembrance upon these mysteries we give her a sign of the gratitude of our hearts, we prove to her that we cannot often enough call to mind the blessings of her unwearied charity in the work of our salvation. From such meditations, which with the frequency of love we awoke in her presence, who may express, who may ever conceive, whatever new joys overflow her ever blessed soul and what tender affections of mercy and of a mother's love arise therein?" (Leo III: Encyclical, *Jucunda semper*, September 8, 1894.)

85. "The unexampled part which the Virgin most admirably played and still plays in the progress; the battles and the triumph of the Catholic faith, makes it evident what God has planned for her to do. It should

fill the hearts of all good people with a firm hope of obtaining those things which are now the object of our common desire. Trust Mary, implore her aid." (Leo XIII: Encyclical, *Adiutricem populi*, September 5, 1895.)

86. "Well may all, shepherds and flocks alike, fly with fullest confidence to the protection of the Blessed Virgin. Let them not fail to call upon her name with one voice, beseeching her as God's mother, publicly and in private by praise, by prayer, by the ardour of their desire: 'Show thyself our Mother.' May her motherly compassion keep her whole family safe from every danger, lead them in the path of genuine prosperity, above all establish them in holy unity." (Leo XIII: Encyclical, *Adiutricem populi*, September 5, 1895.)

87. "May Mary, Queen of the Apostles, who on Calvary took to her mother's heart the care of all humanity, deign to second our undertakings; may she love with an equal tenderness all those who do not know that they have been redeemed by Jesus Christ and all those who happily enjoy the fruits of redemption." (Pius XI: Encyclical, *Rerum Ecclesiae*, February 28, 1926.)

88. "The Virgin's merciful heart sympathises with family needs; she will shower on them that comfort which they miss in the inevitable sorrows of the present life; under her motherly care the joys of the fireside will become for them purer and more peaceful. The holy Virgin not only knows from personal experience a family's heavy burdens; as a tender Mother of Mercy

she strives to lighten the burdens." (Pius XII: Allocution to the newly married, May 10, 1939.)

89. "Since, as St. Bernard declares, 'It is the will of God that we should obtain all favors through Mary,' let everyone hasten to have recourse to Mary. May all mankind bring its petitions, sorrows and anxieties, and lay them on her altar, beseeching her for aid and comfort. And in this present and most grave peril, confidently following the example of our forefathers, let us not fail to do that which, as history testifies, they did with such gratifying results in their days of peril and fearful uncertainty." (Pius XII: Letter to Cardinal Maglione, April 15, 1940.)

90. "The heavenly Child is Mary's heart's delight and the delight of the world; from His kiss springs up that fire of love which makes her Mother of Mercy and magnanimous clemency towards every child of Adam." (Pius XII: Allocution to the pilgrims from Genoa, April 21, 1940.)

91. "Great is Mary's power with God, but great also is her love for us because she is the most loving Mother of all mankind. Therefore, with unwavering faith and fervent love, let every one of us go to Mary, let everyone bring, not only suppliant petitions but in the same way the holy works of penance and charity by which the divine justice, outraged by so many and such heinous sins, may be appeased." (Pius XII: Letter to Cardinal Maglione, April 15, 1942.)

92. "Mary enjoys such power with God, she radi-

ates so much goodness that she can and will support us in our trials." (Pius XII: Letter to Cardinal Villeneuve, September 12, 1945.)

93. "You are adding in remembrance of Mary's favors a precious crown and with it encircling the brow of Our Lady of Fatima. This you are doing in that blessed oasis, fertile ground of the supernatural, where you experience her miraculous patronage very sensibly, and where you feel her Immaculate Heart beating with an immense tenderness and motherly solicitude for you and for all mankind." (Pius XII: Radio message on the occasion of the Coronation of the Statute of Our Lady of Fatima, May 13, 1946.)

94. "To the sad austerity, the sombre terror, the depressing pride of Jansenism, he (St. Louis-Marie de Montfort) opposed the filial, trusting, ardent, expansive and effective love of the devout servant of Mary, towards her who is the refuge of sinners, the Mother of divine grace, our life, our sweetness and our hope. Our advocate, placed between God and the sinner, takes it upon herself to invoke clemency of the judge so as to temper His justice, touch the heart of the sinner and overcome His obstinacy. Convinced by His own personal experience of Mary's role, the missionary declared with a picturesque simplicity all His own that 'never did a sinner resist Him after he had touched His coat collar with the rosary.'" (Pius XII: Allocution at the Canonisation of St. Louis-Marie de Montfort, July 21, 1947.)

Mary moves the Divine Mercy

95. "In Mary, the mystical Ark of the Covenant, the secret mysteries of our reconciliation have been accomplished and the sight of her reminds God of His covenant and causes Him to be mindful of His mercy. Mary is that heavenly stream which brings to the hearts of wretched mortals all God's gifts and graces." (Benedict XIV: Apostolic Constitution, *Gloriosae Dominae*, September 27, 1748.)

Mary is a sign of the Divine Mercy

96. "At Lourdes in France . . . divine mercy manifested itself visibly in the person of the Virgin Mary, the Mediatrix." (St. Pius X: Apostolic Letter, *Summa Deus hominum*, November 27, 1907.)

97. "The Mother of the divine Saviour is now, as in the time of King Achaz, the sign of God's mercy." (Pius XII: Radio message, October 18, 1954.)

Mary is the realization of the Divine Mercy

98. "The plan of this most loving mercy, realized by God in Mary and confirmed by the testament of Christ, was understood with the utmost joy by the holy Apostles and the earliest believers." (Leo XIII: Encyclical, *Octobri mense*, September 22, 1891.)

Mary is the necessary Mediatrix

99. "It is right and proper to affirm that Mary, whom Jesus made His constant companion from the

house of Nazareth to the place of Calvary, knew, as no other knew, the secrets of His Heart, distributes as by a mother's right the treasures of His merits, and is the surest help to the knowledge and love of Christ." (Pius X: Encyclical, *Ad Diem Ilum*, February 2, 1904.)

Mary is the permanent Mediatrix

100. "The recourse we have to Mary in prayer follows upon the office she continually fills by the side of the throne of God as Mediatrix of divine grace, being by worthiness and by merit more acceptable to Him, and for that reason surpassing in power all the Angels and Saints in heaven . . . In the Rosary the part Mary took as our Co-Redemptrix is set before us as though the facts were even then taking place." (Leo XIII: Encyclical, *Jucunda semper*, September 8, 1894.)

Mary's Mediation is motherly and welcoming

101. "Mary is the glorious intermediary. She is the mighty Mother of God. But—what is sweeter—she is gentle, exquisite in tenderness, and of a limitless love and kindness. As such God gave her to us. Having chosen her for the Mother of His only begotten Son, He taught her all a mother's feelings that breathe nothing but pardon and love. Such Christ desired that she should be." (Leo XIII: Encyclical, *Octobri mense*, September 26, 1891.)

102. "Our heart is sad because of those who, although of the household of the Faith, dare to accuse

the devout of excessive or exaggerated veneration towards Mary, gravely offending thereby the filial piety of children toward their Mother." (Leo XIII: Encyclical, *Octobri mense*, September 26, 1891.)

103. "We shall take the opportunity of pointing out the particular ruling and designs of Providence, which ordain that the Rosary should have new power to instil confidence into the hearts of those who pray, and new influence to move the compassionate Heart of our Mother to comfort and generously help us." (Leo XIII: Encyclical *Jucunda semper*, September 18, 1894.)

Mary's Mediation is worthy and pleasant

104. "The Catholic Church has always and with justice put all her hope and trust in the Mother of God. She who is associated with Him in the work of man's salvation has favor and power with her Son greater than any other human or angelic creature has ever obtained or ever can obtain. And, as it is her greatest pleasure to grant her help and comfort to those who seek her, it cannot be doubted that she will deign, even anxiously, to receive the aspirations of the Universal Church." (Leo XIII: Encyclical, *Supreme Apostolatus*, September 1, 1883.)

105. See quotations Nos. 28 and 100 above.

106. See quotation No. 8 above.

Mary's Mediation is faithful and courageous

107. See quotations Nos. 2, 66, 76, 81, 98, 101, 102 above.

Mary's Mediation is powerful

108. "Mary is this glorious intermediary. She is the mighty Mother of God." (Leo XIII: Encyclical, *Octobri mense*, September 22, 1891.)

109. See quotations Nos. 28 and 100 above.

110. "When Mary interposes her powerful protection, the gates of hell cannot prevail. She, in fact, is the most loving and most powerful Mother of God, and of us all, and never was it heard that anyone has had suppliant recourse to her and has not experienced her most efficacious protection. Continue, therefore, as you have been doing, to venerate her with fervent piety, and to love her ardently and to invoke her with these words which you have been accustomed to address to her: 'To you alone has it been given, O most holy and most pure Mother of God, unfailingly to have your petitions ever answered.'" (Pius XII: Apostolic Letter, *Sacro vergente anno*, to the people of Russia, July 7, 1952.)

111. "For a long, long time the people of Poland, with a devotion difficult to equal, have honored and venerated the glorious Queen of countless triumphs, that incomparable Woman adorned with a crown of stars, clothed with the sun, who for us gave birth to the Sun of Justice. In return for her devoted children's testimony of their homage, that Mother of God and

of men, whose bounty matches her power, has often granted graces generously to that people, in a way more clearly recognisable than the dangers amongst which it walked were hidden." (Pius XII: Letter, *Gloriosam Reginam*, to the Polish Bishops, December 8, 1955.)

MARY IS CO-REDEMPTRIX

The relation between Mary and the Redemption

Mary has ties with the Redemption

112. "She who is associated with Him in the work of man's salvation has favor and power with her Son greater than any other human or angelic creature has ever obtained or ever can obtain." (Leo XIII: Encyclical, *Supremi Apostolatus*, September 1, 1883.)

113. "The august Virgin, conceived without original sin, was chosen to be the Mother of Christ in order to be associated with Him in the redemption of mankind." (Pius XI: Letter, *Auspicatus profecto*, to Cardinal Binet, January 28, 1933.)

114. "In this work of redemption the Blessed Virgin Mary was closely associated with Christ and so the sacred liturgy sings: 'Holy Mary, Queen of heaven and Mistress of the world, stood in sorrow at the Cross of Our Lord Jesus Christ.' Wherefore, according to a devout disciple of St. Anselm in the Middle Ages, 'Just as . . . God by His power creating all things is Father and Lord of all, so the Blessed Virgin Mary, restoring all things by her merits, is Mother and Mistress of all;

for God is Lord of all things because by His command He gave them their nature, and Mary is Mistress of all things because she restored them to their original dignity by the grace which she merited.'" (Pius XII: Encyclical, *Ad coeli Reginam*, October 11, 1954.)

Mary begins Redemption

115. "It is impossible to say how pleasing and gratifying to the Blessed Virgin it is when we greet her with the Angelic Salutation, 'full of grace'; and in repeating it do we not fashion these words of praise into a crown of devotion for her? For every time we say them, we recall the memory of her exalted dignity and of the redemption of the human race which God began through her." (Leo XIII: *Magnae Dei Matris*, September 8, 1892.)

Mary cooperates with Redemption

116. "It is impossible to measure the power and scope of her offices since the day she was taken up to that height of heavenly glory in the company of her Son, to which the dignity and lustre of her merits entitle her. From her heavenly abode she began, by God's decree, to watch over the Church, to assist and befriend us as our Mother; so that she who was so intimately associated with the mystery of human salvation is just as closely associated with the distribution of the graces which from all time will flow from the redemption." (Leo XIII: Encyclical, *Adiutricem Populi*, September 5, 1895.)

117. "As the angelic doctor teaches: 'There is no reason why certain others should not be called in a certain way mediators between God and man, that is to say, in so far as they cooperate by predisposing and ministering in the union of man with God' . . . Especially has the Blessed Virgin attained to the glory of this title. For no single individual can ever be imagined who has ever contributed or ever will contribute so much toward reconciling man with God." (Leo XIII: Encyclical, *Fidentem Piumque*, September 20, 1896.)

118. "We naturally turn to the powerful Mother of God. She was the co-operatrix in man's redemption and always the chief and sovereign refuge of Catholics in the trials they underwent." (Leo XIII: Apostolic Constitution, *Ubi primum*, October 2, 1898.)

119. "According to the common teaching of the Doctors, it was God's design that the Blessed Virgin Mary, apparently absent from the public life of Jesus, should assist Him when He was dying nailed to the Cross. Mary suffered and, as it were, nearly died with her suffering Son; for the salvation of mankind she renounced her mother's rights and, as far as it depended on her, offered her Son to placate divine justice; so we may well say that she with Christ redeemed mankind." (Benedict XV: Letter, *Inter sodalicia*, May 22, 1918.)

120. See quotation No. 79 above.

121. "The union between Christ and woman has its greatest charm and most perfect fulfilment in the person of the Virgin Mary . . . It was through the Virgin

Mary that God assumed human nature and joined the race of the sons of Adam. Her dignity as Mother of God brought singular graces and extraordinary privileges upon Mary; preservation from original sin and no personal fault, the splendor of the virtues and the gifts of the Holy Spirit, and intimate participation in all the mysteries of the life of Christ, in His sufferings, in His death and resurrection, in the continuation of His work within the Church, and in His sovereignty over all creatures. All this she was given because she was the Mother of God and because as such she was called upon to play a unique role in the redemption of the world." (Pius XII: Allocution to the World Union of Women's Organisations of Catholic Action, September 29, 1957.)

Mary takes an effective part in Redemption

122. "We are reminded both of Mary's exalted dignity and the graces without number which come to her from God through the 'fruit of her womb'; we recall the other exceptional merits by which she shared with her Son Jesus in man's redemption." (Leo XIII: Apostolic Letter, *Parta humano generi*, September 8, 1901.)

123. "For us nothing can be more effective in winning the Virgin's favor and in meriting the most salutary graces than to surround with the greatest possible honor the mysteries of our redemption in which she not only shared but also took part." (Leo XIII: Apostolic Letter, *Parta humano generi*, September 8, 1901.)

See also quotation No. 45 above.

124. "It was in the presence and under the very gaze of Mary that the divine sacrifice of our redemption was consummated; she took part in it by giving to the world and nourishing the divine Victim, she the Queen of Martyrs." (St. Pius X: Letter, *Ubera cum Fructu*, April 30, 1911.)

125. "The sorrowful Virgin took part with Jesus Christ in the work of the redemption. She was constituted Mother of men, who were confided to her as a testimony of divine love. She took them to herself as sons and she lovingly protects them." (Pius XI: Apostolic Letter, *Explorata res est*, February 2, 1923.)

126. "From the nature of His work, the Redeemer ought to have associated His Mother with His work. For this reason we invoke her under the title of Co-Redemptrix. She gave us the Saviour, she accompanied Him in the work of redemption as far as the Cross itself, sharing with Him the sorrows of the agony and of the death in which Jesus consummated the redemption of mankind. And immediately beneath the Cross, at the last moments of His life, she was proclaimed by the Redeemer, our Mother, the Mother of the whole universe." (Pius XI: Allocution to pilgrims from Vicenza, November 30, 1933.)

Mary by taking part in Redemption redeems mankind

127. "Mary suffered and, as it were, nearly died with her suffering Son; for the salvation of mankind

she renounced her mother's rights and, as far as it depended on her, offered her Son to placate divine justice; so we may well say that she with Christ redeemed mankind." (Benedict XV: Letter, *Inter sodalicia*, May 22, 1918.)

128. "She it was who, immune from all sin, personal or inherited, and ever more closely united with her Son, offered Him on Golgotha to the Eternal Father together with the holocaust of her maternal rights and motherly love and like a new Eve, for all the children of Adam contaminated through this unhappy fall, and thus she, who was the Mother of our head according to the flesh, became by a new title of sorrow and glory the spiritual Mother of His members." (Pius XII: Encyclical, *Mystici corporis*, June 29, 1943.)

Mary is associated with the Redeemer

129. "She who is associated with Him in the work of man's salvation has favor and power with her Son greater than any other human or angelic creature has ever obtained or ever can obtain." (Leo XIII: Encyclical, *Supremi Apostolatus*, September 1, 1883.)

130. "She shared with her Son Jesus in man's redemption." (Leo XIII: Apostolic Letter, *Parta humano generi*, September 8, 1901.)

131. "Since she surpassed all in holiness and union with Christ, and has been associated with Christ in the work of redemption, she, as the expression is, merits *de congruo* what Christ merits *de condigno*, and is the

principal minister in the distribution of grace." (St. Pius X: Encyclical, *Ad diem illum*, February 2, 1904.)

132. "Mother most faithful and most merciful, who as Co-Redemptrix and partaker of thy dear Son's sorrow, didst assist Him as He offered the sacrifice of our redemption on the altar of the Cross." (Pius XI: Radio message to the pilgrims at Lourdes, April 28, 1935.)

133. "The Blessed Virgin Mary is to be called Queen not only on account of her divine motherhood but also because by the will of God she had a great part in the work of our salvation . . . In this work of redemption the Blessed Virgin Mary was closely associated with her Christ . . . Just as Christ, because He redeemed us, is by a special title our King and Lord, so too is Blessed Mary our Queen and our Mistress, because of the unique way in which she cooperated in our redemption. She provided her very substance for His body, she offered Him willingly for us, and she took a unique part in our salvation by desiring it, praying for it, and so obtaining it . . . Mary in the work of redemption was by God's will joined with Jesus Christ, the cause of salvation, in much the same way as Eve was joined with Adam, the cause of death. Hence it can be said that the work of our salvation was brought about by a 'restoration' (St. Irenaeus) in which the human race, just as it was doomed to death by a virgin, was saved by a virgin. She was chosen to be the Mother of Christ in order to have part with Him in the redemption of the human race. She it was who, free from all stain of personal or original sin, always

most closely united with her Son, offered Him up to the Eternal Father on Calvary, along with the sacrifice of her own claim as His Mother and of her own mother love, thus acting as a new Eve on behalf of all Adam's children, ruined by this unhappy fall . . . Just as Christ, the new Adam, is our King not only because He is the Son of God, but also because He is our Redeemer, so also in a somewhat similar manner the Blessed Virgin is Queen not only as Mother of God, but also because she was associated as the second Eve with the new Adam." (Pius XII: Encyclical, *Ad coeli Reginam*, October 11, 1954.)

134. "The most Blessed Virgin Mary was inseparably joined with Christ in accomplishing the work of man's redemption so that our salvation flows from the love of Jesus Christ and His sufferings intimately united with the love and sorrows of His Mother." (Pius XII: Encyclical, *Haurietis aquas*, May 15, 1956.)

Mary is Co-Redemptrix

135. "From the nature of His work the Redeemer ought to have associated His Mother with His work. For this reason we invoke her under the title of Co-Redemptrix. She gave us the Saviour, she accompanied Him in the work of redemption as far as the Cross itself, sharing with Him the sorrows of the agony and of the death in which Jesus consummated the redemption of mankind." (Pius XI: Allocution to pilgrims from Vicenza, November 30, 1933.)

136. See quotations Nos. 69 and 132 above.

MEDIATE OR INDIRECT CO-REDEMPTION

Mary is Mediatrix because she is mother

137. "The eternal Son of God, about to take upon Himself our nature for the saving and ennobling of man, and about to consummate thus a mystical union between Himself and all mankind, did not accomplish His design without obtaining the free consent of her who was to become His Mother. She was the representative of all mankind, according to the illustrious and learned opinion of St. Thomas, who says that 'in the annunciation was awaited the consent of the Virgin standing in the place of humanity.' With equal truth it may be said that of the great treasury of all graces given to us by Our Lord—'for grace and truth came by Jesus Christ'—nothing comes to us except through the mediation of Mary, for such is the will of God. Thus, as no man goes to the Father but by the Son, so no one goes to Christ except through His Mother." (Leo XIII: Encyclical, *Octobri mense*, September 22, 1891.)

138. See quotations Nos. 8, 106 and 117 above.

139. "It was she who gave miraculous birth to Christ Our Lord, adorned already in her virginal womb with the dignity of Head of the Church, and so brought forth the source of all heavenly life." (Pius XII: Encyclical, *Mystici Corporis*, June 29, 1943.)

Mary is Mediatrix because she gives us Christ the Saviour

140. "By thee it was that Jesus Our Saviour and our hope was given unto the world." (Leo XIII: Encyclical, *Amantissimae voluntatis*, April 14, 1895.)

141. See quotations Nos. 8, 106 and 117 above.

142. "To heal the ills of society no remedy is more timely than recourse to her who, having given for the world's salvation the person of her Son, delights in being hailed as the Help of Christians." (Leo XIII: Letter to the Archbishop of Cambrai, July 10, 1903.)

143. "God could have given us the Redeemer of the human race and the founder of the Faith in another way than through the Virgin, but since divine Providence has been pleased that we should have the man-God through Mary, who conceived Him by the Holy Ghost and bore Him in her womb, it only remains for us to receive Christ through the hands of Mary." (St. Pius X: Encyclical, *Ad diem illum*, February 2, 1904.)

144. See quotation No. 10 above.

145. See quotations No. 33 and 71 above.

146. "Whenever we speak of Mary, or speak to her, let us not forget that she is really our Mother, for through her we received divine life. She gave us Jesus, Himself the source of grace. She is the mediatrix and the dispenser of graces." (Pius XII: Radio message to the Italian Catholic Action, December 8, 1953.)

Mary freely consented to the Incarnation

147. "The eternal Son of God, about to take upon Himself our nature . . . did not accomplish His design without obtaining the free consent of her who was to become His Mother." (Leo XIII: Encyclical, *Octobri mense*, September 22, 1891.)

148. "To mankind heading for eternal ruin, she offered a Saviour when she received the announcement of the mystery brought to this earth by the angel, and in giving her consent, gave it in the name of the whole human race." (Leo XIII: Encyclical, *Fidentem piumque*, September 20, 1896.)

149. "She, representing the whole of humanity, gave her consent to a spiritual marriage between the Son of God and human nature." (Pius XII: Encyclical, *Mystici Corporis*, June 29, 1943.)

150. "The maternal office of 'mediatrix' really began at the very moment of her consent to the incarnation; it was manifested for the first time by the first sign of Christ's grace, at Cana in Galilee; from that moment it rapidly spread down through the ages with the growth of the Church." (Pius XII: Apostolic Letter, *Per Christi Matrem*, May 15, 1947.)

151. "The 'fiat' of the Incarnation, her collaboration in the work of her Son, the intensity of the sufferings endured during the passion, and this death of the soul which she experienced on Calvary, had opened the heart of Mary to the universal love of humanity, and

the decision of her divine Son impressed the seal of omnipotence on her motherhood of grace." (Pius XII: Allocution to the Children of Mary, July 17, 1954.)

152. "The origin of Mary's glories, the solemn moment which lights up her whole personality and mission, is that in which she, full of grace, replied to the Archangel Gabriel with '*fiat*' ('Be it done'), expressing her consent to God's plan. Thus did she become the Mother of God and Queen, receiving the royal office of watching over the unity and peace of the human race." (Pius XII: Allocution in St. Peter's Basilica, November 1, 1954.)

Mary gives and prepares the Victim of the sacrifice of Redemption

153. "In a miracle of love, so that she might receive us as her sons, Mary offered generously to the divine justice her own Son, and in her heart died with Him, stabbed by the sword of sorrow." (Leo XIII: Encyclical, *Jucunda semper*, September 8, 1894.)

154. "It was not only the glory of the Mother of God to have presented to God the only begotten who was to be born of human members, the material by which He was prepared as a Victim for the salvation of mankind, but hers also the office of tending and nourishing that Victim, and at the appointed time of offering Him at the altar." (St. Pius X: Encyclical, *Ad diem illum*, February 2, 1904.)

155. "It was in the presence and under the very gaze

of Mary that the divine sacrifice of our redemption was consummated; she took part in it by giving to the world and nourishing the divine Victim, she the Queen of Martyrs." (St. Pius X: Letter, *Ubera cum fructu*, April 30, 1911.)

156. "By her blessed maternity Mary has given us the Redeemer." (Pius XII: Encyclical, *Mediator Dei*, November 20, 1947.)

157. See quotations Nos. 144 and 133 above.

The Body and Blood of Christ were taken from Mary

158. "The blood of Christ shed for our sake, and those members in which He offers to His Father the wounds He received as the price of our liberty are no other than the flesh and blood of the Virgin: 'The flesh of Jesus is the flesh of Mary, and however much it was exalted in the glory of His resurrection, nevertheless the nature of His flesh derived from Mary remained and still remains the same.' (St. Augustine)." (Leo XIII: Encyclical, *Fidentem piumque*, September 20, 1896.)

Mary generates the Author and the Consumer of our faith

159. "If Mary received in her womb Him who is by nature truth Himself in order that 'He, generated in a new order and with a new activity, so invisible in Himself, might become visible in our flesh'; the Son of God made man, being the 'Author and Finisher' of faith, it

surely follows that His most holy Mother should be recognized as sharing in the divine mysteries and as being in a manner the guardian of them, and that upon her as upon a foundation, the noblest after Christ, rises the edifice of the faith of all centuries." (St. Pius X: Encyclical, *Ad diem illum*, February 2, 1904.)

Mary gives us true wisdom

160. "Do not forget that true wisdom is that which she vouchsafed us, that which she teaches us in the name of Wisdom Incarnate. 'Hail, most abundant source from which spring out the streams of divine wisdom, and holds back, with the purest and clearest waters of orthodoxy, the curling waves of error.'" (Pius XII: Radio message to the Marian Congress in Mexico, October 12, 1945.)

Our Lady's Mediation is a source of life and blessing

161. "For this cause do we repeatedly celebrate those glorious titles of Mary's ministry as Mediatrix. We greet her who found favor with God; who was in a signal manner filled with grace by Him so that the superabundance thereof might overflow upon all men; who was united with God by the most intimate of all bonds; who was blessed among women; and who alone took away the curse and bore the blessing—that Fruit of her womb, that happy Fruit in which all the nations of the earth are blessed. We invoke her as Mother of God, and in virtue of a dignity so sublime, what graces

from her may we not promise to ourselves, sinners though we are, in life and in the agonies of death." (Leo XIII: Encyclical, *Jucunda semper*, September 8, 1894.)

162. "The Church does not compare Mary only to the moon; again making use of sacred Scripture, she uses a more vivid figure when exclaiming: 'O Mary, thou art bright as the sun.' Sunlight is far different from moonlight; it is light that warms and vivifies. The moon shines upon the polar icefields, but the icefields remain compact and barren just as darkness and frost endure on moonlit winter nights. Moonlight does not give warmth nor bring life. The sun is the source of light, warmth and life. Now Mary, beautiful as the moon, shines brightly as the sun and irradiates lifegiving warmth. Whenever we speak of her, or speak to her, let us not forget that she is really our Mother, for through her we received divine life. She gave us Jesus, Himself the source of grace. Mary is the Mediatrix and dispenser of graces." (Pius XII: Radio message to the Italian Catholic Action, December 8, 1953.)

Mary is the Mother of Christ for our salvation

163. "The Virgin was kept immune from all stain of original sin because she was to be the Mother of Christ, and she was the Mother of Christ that the hope of everlasting happiness might be born again in our souls." (St. Pius X: Encyclical, *Ad diem illum*, February 2, 1904.)

Mary was Mediatrix in the stable at Bethlehem

164. "No one can fail to be sweetly affected when considering who . . . presented her Son to the shepherds, to the kings and to Simeon." (Leo XIII: Encyclical, *Fidentem piumque*, September 20, 1896.)

Mary is Mediatrix at the Visitation

165. "St. John the Baptist, by a singular privilege, is sanctified in His mother's womb and favored with special graces, that he may prepare the way of the Lord, and this comes to pass by the greeting of Mary, who had been inspired to visit her cousin." (Leo XIII: Encyclical, *Jucunda semper*, September 8, 1894.)

166. "No one can fail to be sweetly affected when considering who appeared in the house of Elizabeth as the minister of the divine gifts." (Leo XIII: Encyclical, *Fidentem piumque*, September 20, 1896.)

167. "The only begotten Son of God at all times paid to His most holy Mother most evident marks of honor . . . He associated her with Himself in each of His first two miracles—the miracle of grace when, at the salutation of Mary, the infant leaped in the womb of Elizabeth; the miracle of nature when He turned water into wine at the marriage feast of Cana." (Leo XIII: Encyclical, *Augustissimae*, September 12, 1897.)

Our Lady is Mediatrix at Cana

168. See last quotation above.

169. "The maternal office of mediatrix really began at the very moment of her consent to the Incarnation;

it was manifested for the first time by the first sign of Christ's grace, at Cana in Galilee; from that moment it rapidly spread down through the ages with the growth of the Church." (Pius XII: Apostolic Letter, *Per Christi Matrem*, May 15, 1947.)

MARY AT THE CROSS

Mary accompanied Christ at the foot of the Cross in His work of Redemption

170. "We invoke her under the title of Co-Redemptrix. She gave us the Saviour, she accompanied Him in the work of redemption as far as the Cross itself, sharing with Him the sorrows and the agony and of the death in which Jesus consummated the redemption of mankind. And immediately beneath the Cross, at the last moments of His life, she was proclaimed by the Redeemer our Mother, the Mother of the whole universe." (Pius XI: Allocution to pilgrims from Vicenza, November 30, 1933.)

Mary acquires every grace because of her participation at the Cross

171. "If the graces which we receive from the treasury of redemption are distributed, so to speak, by the hands of the sorrowful Virgin, no one can deny that the grace of a happy death must come from Mary because, in fact, it is by means of this pre-eminent grace that the work of redemption reaches its fulfilment in every

man. In the same way, the sorrowful Virgin was constituted by Jesus Christ as the Mother of all men, and as she received them as a heritage from the infinite love of Jesus, she assumed with maternal love the duty of watching over their spiritual life—it is evident that she cannot do other than help most devotedly her dearest adopted sons at the hour at which it is necessary to secure for them salvation and sanctity for all eternity." (Benedict XV: Letter, *Inter sodalicia*, May 22, 1918.)

172. "Her dignity as Mother of God brought singular graces and extraordinary privileges upon Mary . . . an intimate participation in all the mysteries of the life of Christ, in His sufferings, in His death and resurrection, in the continuation of His work in the Church, and in His sovereignty over all creatures. All this she was given because she was the Mother of God, and because as such she was called upon to play a unique role in the redemption of the world." (Pius XII.)

Mary is Co-Redemptrix because of her union with her crucified Son

173. "She will reach a height of glory granted to no other creature, whether human or angelic, because no one will be able to be compared to her in virtue and in merit; she will be Queen of Heaven and of earth, for she will be the invincible Queen of Martyrs. She will be seated in the heavenly city of God by the side of her Son, crowned for all eternity, because she will drink with Him the cup overflowing with sorrow, faith-

fully through all her life, most faithfully on Calvary." (Leo XIII: Encyclical, *Magnae Dei Matris*, September 8, 1892.)

Mary is Co-Redemptrix because she united her sufferings with those of her Son

174. "It is certain that she suffered in the very depths of her soul with His most bitter sufferings and His torments. It was before the eyes of Mary that the divine sacrifice for which she had borne and nurtured the Victim was to be finished. As we contemplate Him in the last and most piteous of these mysteries we see that 'there stood by the Cross of Jesus, Mary His Mother,' who, in a miracle of love, so that she might receive us as her sons, offered generously to Divine Justice her own Son, and in her heart died with Him, stabbed by the sword of sorrow." (Leo XIII: Encyclical, *Jucunda semper*, September 8, 1894.)

175. "O Holy Mother of God, to thee we lift our prayers, for thou, powerful and merciful, are the mediatrix of our salvation. Oh, by the sweetness of the joys that come to thee by thy sweet Son Jesus, by thy participation in His ineffable sorrows, by the splendors of His glory shining in thee, we earnestly beseech thee, listen, have pity on us, hear us." (Leo XIII: Encyclical, *Jucunda semper*, September 8, 1894.)

176. See quotations Nos. 126 and 170 above.

177. "Look at the holy and immaculate Mother; she holds in her lap the lifeless body of her divine Son.

Could you possibly imagine that the sorrowful Mother would murmur against God? That she would ask the reason for such suffering? We would not have been redeemed, if that Mother had not seen her Son die in torment and there would not have been for us any possibility of salvation." (Pius XII: Radio message to the Sick, February 14, 1954.)

178. "This manifestation of your devotion to the most pure heart of the Virgin Mary, seat of that love, of that sorrow, of those most sublime affections which have so great a part in our redemption, especially when she kept vigil at the foot of the Cross, doubtless merits attention." (Pius XII: Radio message to the Spanish Marian Congress, October 12, 1954.)

179. "By the will of God, the most Blessed Virgin Mary was inseparably joined with Christ in accomplishing the work of man's redemption, so that our salvation flows from the love of Jesus Christ and His sufferings intimately united with the love and sorrows of His Mother." (Pius XII: Encyclical, *Haurietis aquas*, May 15, 1956.)

Mary, Co-Redemptrix through her tears

180. "Travelling the road which the divine Blood of Christ and Mary's tears have consecrated, we are certain to attain without trouble to a share in her blessed glory." (Leo XIII: Encyclical, *Magnae Dei Matris*, September 8, 1892.)

181. "We are inspired by the certainty that your

eyes, which wept over the earth crimsoned by the Blood of Jesus, are yet turned towards this world racked by wars and persecutions, the oppression of the just and the weak." (Pius XII: Allocution to pilgrims in St. Peter's Square, November 1, 1950.)

182. "It is true that up to the present this apostolic See has not in any way made known its judgment concerning the tears which are said to have been shed by an image of her in the humble house of some working men. Nevertheless it was with lively emotion that we read the unanimous declaration of the Episcopate of Sicily of the reality of the event. Without doubt Mary is eternally happy in heaven and suffers neither pain nor sadness. And yet, she does not there remain insensible, but rather feels love and pity for the suffering human race, to which she was given as a Mother when she stood, sad and weeping, at the foot of the Cross, to which her Son was nailed. Will men understand the mysterious language of those tears? Oh, the tears of Mary! On Golgotha they were tears of compassion for her Jesus and of sadness for the sins of the world. Does she still weep for the wounds produced anew in the Mystical Body of Jesus? Or does she weep for her many sons, whose errors and sins have extinguished the life of grace and gravely offend the divine Majesty? Or are they tears of expectation for the delayed return of her other children, once faithful, and now led astray by mirages into the ranks of God's enemies?" (Pius XII: Radio message to the Marian Congresses of Sicily, October 17, 1954.)

183. "The Virgin wept. Her tears were first prophesied by holy Simeon's words and later forcibly fulfilled even to the letter, in that woman who stood beneath the Cross of her divine Son. Those tears obtain for us grace and salvation." (Pius XII: Radio message to the faithful of Ecuador, April 22, 1956.)

Mary is Co-Redemptrix because of her charity and her heart

184. "Jesus is nailed to the Cross and He is reproached with maledictions 'for having made Himself the Son of God.' But she unceasingly recognized and adored the divinity in Him. She bore His dead body to the tomb, but never for the moment doubted that He would rise again. Then the love of God with which she burned made her a partaker in the sufferings of Christ and the associate of His Passion; with Him, moreover, as if forgetful of her own sorrow, she prayed for the pardon of the executioners although they in their hate cried out: 'His blood be upon us and upon our children.'" (St. Pius X: Encyclical, *Ad diem illum*, February 2, 1904.)

185. "Practise Mary's virtues: the charm of her Immaculate Heart; her recollection and spirit of prayer . . . ; the love of God, humble, ardent and joyous, which shines forth in the Magnificat; the love of others as well, of all, her relatives, her friends, all men—that incomparable charity which makes her fly to the service of her cousin Elizabeth as soon as she learns of

her approaching motherhood, which makes her attentive to the plight of the bridal couple when the wine begins to fail at the marriage feast of Cana, which at the end unites her so sorrowfully and so profoundly to the sufferings of her divine Son for the salvation of the human race." (Pius XII: Radio message to pilgrims at the shrine of St. Anne of Auray, July 26, 1954.)

186. "The most pure heart of Mary, seat of that love, of that sorrow, of those most sublime affections which had so great a part in our redemption, especially when she kept vigil at the foot of the Cross." (Pius XII: Radio message to the Spanish Marian Congress, October 12, 1954.)

Mary is Co-Redemptrix because she dies with Jesus

187. "She took her part in the painful expiation offered by her Son for the sins of the world. She suffered in the very depths of her soul with His most bitter sufferings and with His torments. It was before the eyes of Mary that the divine sacrifice for which she had borne and nurtured the Victim was to be finished . . . In the miracle of love, so that she might receive us as her sons, she offered generously to the divine justice her own Son and in her heart died with Him, stabbed by the sword of sorrow." (Leo XIII: Encyclical, *Jucunda semper*, September 8, 1894.)

188. "According to the common teaching of the Doctors it was God's design that the Blessed Virgin

Mary, apparently absent from the public life of Jesus, should assist Him when He was dying nailed to the Cross. Mary suffered and as it were nearly died with her suffering Son; for the salvation of mankind she renounced her mother's rights and, as far as it depended on her, offered her Son to placate divine justice; so we may well say that she with Christ redeemed mankind." (Benedict XV: Letter, *Inter sodalicia*, May 22, 1918.)

By means of the union with her Son, Mary is Reparatrix

189. "May the most gracious Mother of God, who gave us Jesus as Redeemer, who reared Him, and at the foot of the Cross offered Him a Victim, who by her mysterious union with Christ and by her matchless grace rightly merits the name Reparatrix . . . Christ Our Lord, who though sole Mediator between God and man, wished to make His Mother the advocate for sinners and the dispenser and mediatrix of His grace." (Pius XI: Encyclical, *Miserentissimus Redemptor*, May 8, 1928.)

By means of union with her Son's sufferings, Mary is the cause of salvation

190. "Fly with greater confidence to the Mother of God. There the Christian people have always sought chief refuge at the hour of danger, because 'she has been constituted the cause of salvation for the whole human race.' (St. Irenaeus)" (Pius XII: Encyclical, *Ingruentium malorum*, September 15, 1951.)

Mary shared the agony and death in which her Son consummated Redemption

191. "We invoke her under the title of Co-Redemptrix. She gave us the Saviour; she accompanied Him in the work of redemption as far as the Cross itself, sharing with Him the sorrows of the agony and of the death in which Jesus consummated the redemption of mankind." (Pius XI: Allocution to pilgrims from Vicenza, November 30, 1933.)

Mary presents the Victim of salvation

192. "It was not only the glory of the Mother of God to have presented to God the only begotten who was to be born of human members the material by which she was prepared as a victim for the salvation of mankind, but hers also the office of tending and nourishing that Victim, and at the appointed time of offering Him at the altar." (St. Pius X: Encyclical, *Ad diem illum*, February 2, 1904.)

193. See quotations Nos. 10, 144 and 189 above.

194. "She . . . ever most closely united with her Son, offered Him on Golgotha to the Eternal Father together with the holocaust of her maternal rights and motherly love, like a new Eve, for all the children of Adam contaminated through His unhappy fall, and thus she, who was the Mother of our head according to the flesh, became by a new title of sorrow and glory the spiritual Mother of all His members." (Pius XII: Encyclical, *Mystici Corporis*, June 29, 1943.)

Mary offers her Son for us to the Divine Justice

195. "She stood at the foot of the Cross and offered those sorrows to the Eternal Father for our salvation." (Pius VII: Letter, *Id officii debent*, January 9, 1801.)

196. "At the foot of the Cross she offered up her whole self with her child Jesus—then and thereafter she took her part in the painful expiation offered by her Son for the sins of the world . . . In a miracle of love, so that she might receive us as her sons, she offered generously to Divine Justice her own Son, and in her heart died with Him, stabbed by the sword of sorrow." (Leo XIII Encyclical, *Jucunda semper*, September 8, 1894.)

197. "Mary suffered and, as it were, nearly died with her suffering Son; for the salvation of mankind she renounced her mother's rights and, as far as it depended on her, offered her Son to placate Divine Justice; so we may well say that she with Christ redeemed mankind." (Benedict XV: Letter, *Inter sodalicia*, May 22, 1918.)

198. See quotations Nos. 128 and 194 above.

199. "She it was, who, always most closely united with her Son, offered Him up to the Eternal Father on Calvary, along with the sacrifice of her own claims as His Mother and of her own mother love." (Pius XII: Encyclical, *Ad coeli Reginam*, October 11, 1954.)

Mary gives herself as Mother and Mediatrix

200. See quotations Nos. 2, 13, 76 and 101 above.

Mary offers her love and her maternal rights

201. See quotations Nos. 119 and 197 above.

202. "The graces which we receive from the treasury of redemption are distributed, so to speak, by the hands of the sorrowful Virgin . . . The sorrowful Virgin was constituted by Jesus Christ as Mother of all men, and as she received them as a heritage from the infinite love of Jesus, she assumed with maternal love the duty of watching over their spiritual life . . . the faithful also cherish the firm belief, supported by long experience, that all those who seek Mary's protection will be saved for all eternity." (Pope Benedict XV: Letter, *Inter sodalicia*, May 22, 1918.)

203. See quotations Nos. 128, 194 and 198 above.

204. See quotations Nos. 133 and 199 above.

Mary is willingly present at the sacrifice of the Redeemer

205. See quotations Nos. 153, 174, 187 and 196 above.

206. "It was in the presence and under the very gaze of Mary that the divine sacrifice of our redemption was consummated; she took part in it by giving to the world and nourishing the divine Victim, she the Queen of Martyrs." (St. Pius X: Letter, *Ubera cum fructu*, April 30, 1911.)

207. See quotations Nos. 119, 188, 197 and 201 above.

Mary offered her sacrifice of Mother

208. "After witnessing at the foot of the Cross the awful spectacle of the Passion of Our Lord, in which she had offered the most difficult sacrifice that could be asked of a mother, she continued to lavish her maternal care upon the first Christian adopted children." (Pius XII: Allocution in St. Peter's Basilica, November 1, 1954.)

From the Annunciation to Calvary, Mary intimately united herself to the sacrifice of her Son

209. "She was so closely united to the sacrifice of her divine Son, from the virginal conception of Jesus Christ to His sorrowful Passion, that she was called by some Fathers of the Church, Virgin Priest." (Pius IX: Letter, *Cum purgaturus*, August 25, 1873.)

Mary, through her merits, takes part in the Redemption

210. "The recourse we have to Mary in prayer follows upon the office she continually fills by the side of the throne of God as Mediatrix of divine grace, being by worthiness and by merit more acceptable to Him, and for that reason surpassing in power all the angels and saints in heaven." (Leo XIII: Encyclical, *Jucunda semper*, September 8, 1894.)

211. "We recall the other exceptional merits by which she shared with her Son Jesus in man's redemp-

tion." (Leo XIII: Apostolic Letter, *Parta Humano Generi*, September 8, 1901.)

212. "Mary is mistress of all things because she restored them to their original dignity by the grace which she merited." (Pius XII: Encyclical, *Ad coeli Reginam*, October 11, 1954.)

Mary takes part in the Redemption in a manner proportionate to her sanctity and her union with Christ

213. "We are . . . very far from declaring the Mother of God to be the authoress of supernatural grace. Grace comes from God alone. But since she surpassed all in holiness and union with Christ and has been associated with Christ in the work of redemption, she, as the expression is, merits *de congruo* what Christ merits *de condigno*, and is the principal minister in the distribution of grace." (St. Pius X: Encyclical, *Ad diem illum*, February 2, 1904.)

Mary merits "de congruo" what Christ merits "de condigno"

214. See last quotation.

Mary completes the Passion of Christ more than all other creatures

215. "She, finally, true Queen of Martyrs, by bearing with courageous and confident heart her immense weight of sorrows, more than all Christians, 'filled up

those things that are wanting of the sufferings of Christ for His Body which is the Church.' " (Pius XII: Encyclical, *Mystici Corporis*, June 29, 1943.)

Mary gathers the heritage of work which her Son left her

216. "As such (i.e. gentle, exquisite in tenderness, and of a limitless love and kindness) she proves herself by her courage in gathering the heritage of the enormous labours of her dying Son in accepting freely the office of Mother towards us all." (Leo XIII: Encyclical, *Octobri mense*, September 22, 1891.)

On the Cross, Christ confirms this divine plan on Mary

217. "She is the mighty Mother of God. But—what is still sweeter—she is gentle, exquisite in tenderness, and of limitless love and kindness . . . As such Christ proclaimed her from the Cross when He entrusted to her care and love the whole of the race of man in the person of His disciple John." (Leo XIII: Encyclical, *Octobri mense*, September 22, 1891.)

MARY, DISPENSER OF GRACE

She takes part in the distribution of grace

Mary fulfils her office of Mother in the Cenacle

218. "With a generous heart Mary undertook and discharged the duties of her high but laborious office,

the beginnings of which were consecrated in the Cenacle. With wonderful care she nurtured the first Christians by her holy example, her authoritative counsel, her sweet consolation, her fruitful prayers. She was, in very truth, the Mother of the Church, the teacher and queen of the Apostles, to whom, besides, she confided no small part of the divine mysteries which she kept in her heart." (Leo XIII. Encyclical, *Adiutricem populi*, September 5, 1895.)

Mary Reparatrix

219. "From this community of will and suffering between Christ and Mary she merited to become most worthily the Reparatrix of the lost world." (St. Pius X: Encyclical, *Ad diem illum*, February 2, 1904.)

220. See quotations Nos. 171 and 202 above.

Mary is Mediatrix in the distribution of grace

221. "God has committed to her the treasury of all good things, in order that everyone may know that through her are obtained every hope, every grace, and all salvation. For this is His will, that we obtain everything through Mary." (Pius IX: Encyclical *Ubi primum*, February 2, 1849.)

222. "As such He proclaimed her from the Cross when He entrusted to her care and love the whole of the race of man in the person of His disciple John. And as such does she prove herself by her courage in gathering the heritage of the enormous labours of her dying

Son, in accepting freely the office of Mother towards us all." (Leo XIII: Encyclical, *Octobri mense*, September 22, 1891.)

223. "The recourse we have to Mary in prayer follows upon the office she continually fills by the side of the throne of God as Mediatrix of divine grace." (Leo XIII: Encyclical, *Jucunda semper*, September 8, 1894.)

224. "The power thus put in her hands is all but unlimited. How unerringly right, then, are Christian souls when they turn to Mary for help as though impelled by an instinct of nature, confidently sharing with her their future hopes and past achievements, their sorrows and joys, commending themselves like children to the care of a bountiful mother. How rightly, too, has every nation and every liturgy without exception acclaimed her great renown, which has grown greater with the voice of each succeeding century. Among her many other titles we find her hailed as 'Our Lady,' 'Our Mediatrix,' 'The Reparatrix of the whole world,' 'The Dispenser of all heavenly gifts.'" (Leo XIII: Encyclical, *Adiutricem populi*, September 5, 1895.)

225. "Especially has the Blessed Virgin a claim to the glory of this title (i.e. Mediatrix). For no single individual can ever be imagined who has contributed or ever will contribute so much towards reconciling man with God. To mankind, heading for eternal ruin, she offered a Saviour when she received the announcement of the mystery brought to this earth by the Angel, and

in giving her consent made it in the name of the whole human race. She it is from whom Jesus is born; she is therefore truly His Mother and for this reason a worthy and acceptable Mediatrix to the Mediator." (Leo XIII: Encyclical, *Fidentem piumque*, September 20, 1896.)

226. "From this community of will and suffering between Christ and Mary she merited to become most worthily the Reparatrix of the lost world and dispensatrix of all the gifts that our Saviour purchased for us by His death and by His Blood . . . By this union of sorrow and suffering which existed between the Mother and the Son, it has been allowed to the august Virgin to be the most powerful Mediatrix and advocate of the whole world with her divine Son." (St. Pius X: Encyclical, *Ad diem illum*, February 2, 1904.)

227. "It is by means of her, of her who is the mirror of justice and the seat of wisdom, that Almighty God ordained that we should receive everything." (St. Pius X: Allocution, November 12, 1910.)

228. "If in every miracle we must recognise the mediation of Mary by means of whom according to the divine will all graces and favors come to us, no one can deny that in one of the miracles approved by us this mediation of the Blessed Virgin has been manifested in a very special manner." (Benedict XV: Allocution, April 6, 1919.)

229. "Mary is all powerful with her divine Son who grants all graces to mankind through her." (Benedict XV: Encyclical, *Fausto appetente die*, June 29, 1921.)

230. "Trusting in her intercession with Christ Our Lord, who . . . . wished to make His Mother the advocate for sinners and the dispenser and mediatrix of His grace." (Pius XI: Encyclical, *Miserentissimus Redemptor*, May 8, 1928.)

231. "God alone gives grace according to the measure which in His infinite wisdom He foresees but, though that grace comes from God, it is given through Mary, our advocate and mediatrix, since motherly affection on the one hand finds response in filial devotion on the other." (Pius XI: Allocution, August 15, 1933.)

232. "Queen of the Most Holy Rosary, Help of Christians, Refuge of Mankind, triumphant in all battles for God! We, your suppliants, prostrate ourselves at your throne, confident that we shall obtain mercy and receive grace, the needed assistance and protection, during the calamities of these days, not indeed by our own merits, of which we presume nothing, but solely through the immense goodness of your motherly heart." (Pius XII: Radio message, October 31, 1942.)

233. "May she be blessed whom he constituted mother of mercy, queen and our most loving advocate, mediatrix of His graces, dispenser of His treasures!" (Pius XII: Radio message, May 13, 1946.)

234. "She is associated with Him for ever, with power so to speak infinite, in the distribution of the graces which flow from redemption." (Pius XII: Radio message for the crowning of the statue of Our Lady of Fatima, May 13, 1946.)

235. "She is our kindest Mother, who has shown herself always, in the face of every danger, our powerful helper and channel of grace." (Pius XII: Encyclical, *Auspicia quaedam*, May 1, 1948.)

236. "She gave us Jesus, Himself the source of grace. Mary is the mediatrix and dispenser of graces." (Pius XII: Radio message to the Italian Catholic Action, December 8, 1953.)

237. "She has been appointed the mediatrix of all the graces which look towards sanctification." (Pius XII: Apostolic Constitution, *Sedes sapientiae*, May 31, 1956.)

Mary is Mediatrix of all Mediators

238. "It is necessary to postulate the intercession of her who the Holy Father greeted as 'Mediatrix Mediatorum omnium.'" (Bishop of Orleans to pilgrims for canonization of Joan of Arc, April 6, 1919.)

Mary is minister of graces

239. "During times of great trouble, pastors and the faithful were always accustomed to invoke with confidence the glorious Mother of God, the most powerful help of Christians, in whose hands all graces are placed." (Leo XIII: Letter to the Bishops of Italy, September 20, 1887.)

240. "With equal truth it may be said that of the great treasury of all graces given to us by Our Lord . . . nothing comes to us except through the mediation of

Mary, for such is the will of God." (Leo XIII: Encyclical, *Octobri mense*, September 22, 1891.)

241. "None, O Mother of God, attains salvation except through thee, none receives a gift from the throne of mercy except through thee." (Leo XIII: Encyclical: *Adiutricem populi*, September 5, 1895.)

242. "Mary . . . is the principal minister in the distribution of grace." (St. Pius X: Encyclical, *Ad diem illum*, February 2, 1904.)

243. "Mary is all powerful with her divine Son who grants all graces to mankind through her . . . The Church is in the habit of greeting the Virgin as Mother of Grace and Mother of Mercy." (Benedict XV: Encyclical, *Fausto appetente die*, June 29, 1921.)

244. "From whom can we expect the salvation of the Christian people today if not from her of whom it is written that whosoever shall find her shall find life and shall have salvation from the Lord?" (Pius XI: Letter, *Cum valde*, February 20, 1929.)

245. "The Mother of God, minister of heavenly graces, was placed at the zenith of power and of glory in heaven to give the help of her patronage to men searching their way on earth among many fatigues and dangers." (Pius XI: Letter, *Sollemne semper*, August 15, 1932.)

246. "The grace of Christ comes to us through the Mother of Christ. She . . . became at the same time Mother of Christ and Mother of Divine Grace. The

maternal office of mediatrix really began at the very moment of her consent to the Incarnation." (Pius XII: Apostolic Letter, *Per Christi Matrem*, May 15, 1947.)

Mary is the dispenser of graces

247. "There can be no shorter and more efficacious means to this end (seeking for help from heaven) than by obtaining through devotion and piety the favor of the Virgin Mary, the Mother of God, the guardian of our peace and the minister to us of heavenly grace, who is placed on the highest summit of power and glory in heaven, in order that she may bestow the help of her patronage on men." (Leo XIII: Encyclical, *Supremi Apostolatus*, September 1, 1883.)

248. "We have a confident hope that God will at length let Himself be moved and have pity upon the state of His Church, and give ear to the prayers coming to Him through her whom He has chosen to be the dispenser of all heavenly graces." (Leo XIII: Encyclical, *Superiore Anno*, August 30, 1884.)

249. "Thus is confirmed the law of merciful mediation of which we have spoken, and which St. Bernardine of Siena thus expresses: 'Every grace granted to men has three successive steps: By God it is communicated to Christ, from Christ it passes to the Virgin, and from the Virgin it descends to us.'" (Leo XIII: Encyclical, *Jucunda semper*, September 8, 1894.)

250. "From her heavenly abode, she began, by God's decree, to watch over the Church, to assist and befriend

us as our Mother; so that she who was so intimately associated with the mystery of human salvation is just as closely associated with the distribution of the graces which from all time will flow from the redemption." (Leo XIII: Encyclical, *Adiutricem populi*, September 5, 1895.)

251. "It is right and proper to affirm that Mary . . . distributes as by a mother's right the treasures of His merits and is the surest help to the knowledge and love of Christ." (St. Pius X: Encyclical, *Ad diem illum*, February 2, 1904.)

252. "All the graces which God deigns to bestow in pity upon men are dispensed through the most holy Virgin." (Benedict XV: Letter of May 5, 1917.)

253. "Trusting in her intercession with Christ Our Lord, who wished to make His Mother the advocate for sinners and the dispenser and mediatrix of His grace . . ." (Pius XI: Encyclical, *Miserentissimus Redemptor*, May 8, 1928.)

254. "To Mary, who reigns in heaven, humble yet higher than any creature, near His throne, God grants the custody of the treasures of His manifold graces. She is, moreover, their minister and generous dispenser." (Pius XII: Allocution, April 21, 1940.)

255. "May she be blessed whom he constituted . . . dispenser of His treasures." (Pius XII: Radio message, May 13, 1946.)

Mary is distributor of graces

256. "Mary is that heavenly stream which brings to the hearts of wretched mortals all God's gifts and graces." (Benedict XIV: Apostolic Constitution, *Gloriosae Dominae*, September 27, 1748.)

257. "She is associated with Him for ever, with power so to speak infinite, in the distribution of the graces which flow from redemption." (Pius XI: Radio message, May 13, 1946.)

258. "Mary is the mediatrix and dispenser of graces." (Pius XII: Radio message, December 8, 1953.)

259. "She has her royal power to distribute the treasures of the kingdom of the divine Redeemer." (Pius XII: Encyclical, *Ad coeli Reginam*, October 11, 1954.)

260. "She never ceases to bestow all the treasures of her affection and loving attention upon a humanity so much in need of compassion." (Pius XII: Allocution, November 1, 1954.)

261. "The Mother of God, your Queen . . . is the mediatrix and dispenser of reward for your every conquest." (Pius XII: Letter, *Gloriosam Reginam*, December 8, 1955.)

Mary is the treasurer of graces

262. "The Virgin Mother of God in person, before God treasurer of all graces, by her repeated apparitions seemed to approve and confirm the devotion of the French people." (Pius XI: Apostolic Letter, *Galliam Ecclesiae filiam*, March 2, 1922.)

263. "To Mary . . . God grants the custody of the treasures of His manifold graces." (Pius XII: Allocution, April 21, 1940.)

264. "While Peter has the keys of heaven, Mary has the key to God's heart; while Peter binds and looses, Mary also binds with the chains of love and looses with the gift of pardon. While Peter is the guardian and the minister of indulgences, Mary is the generous and wise treasurer of God's favors. 'He who desires grace and does not have recourse to Mary, desires to fly without wings.' (Dante)." (Pius XII: Allocution, April 21, 1940.)

265. "Hail, most abundant source from which spring out the streams of divine wisdom, and holds back, with the purest and clearest waters of orthodoxy, the curling waves of error." (Pius XII: Radio message, October 12, 1945.)

266. See quotation No. 259 above.

Mary administers graces

267. "To Mary, who reigns in heaven, humble yet higher than any creature, near His throne, God grants the custody of the treasures of His manifold graces. She is, moreover, their minister and generous dispenser." (Pius XII: Allocution, April 21, 1940.)

Mary showers graces on every social class

268. "The queenship of Mary can suggest to rulers of nations attitudes and counsels corresponding to the needs of our day. But she does not neglect others, never

ceasing to pour forth upon all the peoples of the earth and upon all classes of society the abundance of her graces." (Pius XII: Allocution, November 1, 1954.)

Mary distributes graces without exception of persons

269. "She does not discriminate between noble and princely palaces and the lowly thatched cottage. If she feels at all partial it is toward the poor and miserable, the sorrowful and the unhappy, towards all who in this vale of tears shed also their own; souls whom misfortune casts down, whom sin and remorse humiliate; whom prayer comforts, repentance regenerates and graces make children of Mary in likeness to her own Son." (Pius XII: Allocution, April 21, 1940.)

The three stages of the distribution of graces are from God the Father to Christ, from Christ to Mary, and from Mary to us

270. See quotation No. 249 above.

Mary makes us a present of her superabundant fullness

271. "She is instantly at our side of her own accord, even though she has not been invoked. She dispenses grace with a generous hand from what treasure with which from the beginning she was divinely endowed in fullest abundance that she might be worthy to be the Mother of God. By the fullness of grace which confers on her the most illustrious of her many titles, the

Blessed Virgin is infinitely superior to all the hierarchies of men and angels, the creature who is closest of all to Christ. It is a great thing in any saint to have grace sufficient for the salvation of many souls; but to have enough to suffice for the salvation of everybody in the world is the greatest of all; and this is found in Christ and in the Blessed Virgin." (Leo XIII: Encyclical, *Magnae Dei Matris*, September 8, 1892.)

"272. We repeatedly celebrate those glorious titles of her ministry as mediatrix. Her do we greet who found favor with God, who was in a signal manner filled with grace by Him so that the superabundance thereof might overflow upon all men." (Leo XIII: Encyclical, *Jucunda semper*, September 8, 1894.)

273. "If we consider ever so little how many and powerful are the reasons which prompt this holy Mother to bestow on us these precious gifts, oh, how our hopes will be expanded." (St. Pius X, Encyclical, *Ad diem illum*, February 2, 1904.)

Mary is the channel of graces

274. "Mary is that heavenly stream which brings to the hearts of wretched mortals all God's gifts and graces." (Benedict XIV, Apostolic Constitution, *Gloriosae dominae*, September 27, 1748.)

275. See quotation No. 249 above.

276. "Are not Jesus and Mary the two sublime loves of the Christian people? . . One of them is the source and the other the channel of grace for giving us a new

birth into spiritual life." (Pius XII: Allocution, April 21, 1940.)

277. "Pope Leo XIII proclaimed that almost unlimited power was given to the Blessed Virgin Mary in distributing graces and St. Pius X added that Mary undertakes this office as by a mother's right." (Pius XII: Encyclical, *Ad coeli Reginam*, October 11, 1954.)

278. "She is the crystal-pure channel, not the fountain, of that superabundant divine grace you beg through her immaculate heart for home and Church and country." (Pius XII: Radio message, December 8, 1956.)

Mary is the neck-channel of grace

279. "Mary, as St. Bernard justly remarks, is the 'aqueduct,' or if you will, the neck by which the body is joined to the head, and the head transmits to the body its power and virtue: 'For she is the neck of our head, by which He communicated to His mystical body all His spiritual gifts.'" (St. Pius X: Encyclical, *Ad diem illum*, February 2, 1904.)

All good comes from Mary

280. "May God, who in His most merciful providence gave us this mediatrix, and decreed that all good should come to us by the hands of Mary' . . ." (Leo XIII: Encyclical, *Jucunda semper*, September 8, 1894.)

281. "It is God's will that through her, His own Mother, we have all things; in His supreme goodness

He has constituted her the unerring support of Christianity." (Leo XIII: Letter to the Archbishop of Turin, August 2, 1898.)

282. See quotations Nos. 171, 203, 221 above.

283. "We know that every blessing that comes to us from the Almighty God comes to us through the hands of Our Lady." (Pius XI: Encyclical, *Ingravescentibus malis*, September 29, 1937.)

Mary intervenes in all concessions of grace

284. "Though grace comes from God, it is given through Mary, our advocate and mediatrix, since motherly affection on the one hand finds response in filial devotion on the other." (Pius XI: Allocution, August 15, 1933.)

285. "Think over the story of your own lives. Do you not notice in them a pattern of the graces received from God? You are then able to add the thought, 'Mary took a part in the granting of such graces.' Flowers bloomed and fruits ripened in my life, thanks to the warming influence of the woman who is 'bright as the sun.'" (Pius XII: Radio message. December 8, 1953.)

God uses Mary to fulfil every miracle

286. See quotation No. 167 above.

287. "In every miracle we must recognise the mediation of Mary." (Benedict XV: Allocution, April 6, 1919.)

MARY IS MEDIATRIX WITH HER PRAYER

288. "Mary is our Mother, the Mother of Pity and Grace, the Mother of Mercy, to whom Christ Our Lord in His dying breath on the Cross entrusted us, in order that, as He implores His heavenly Father for us, she may likewise entreat her Son on our behalf." (Pius VIII: Apostolic Constitution, *Praesentissimum sane*, March 3, 1830.)

289. We hasten with fervent zeal to implore the divine aid through the maternal intercession of the ever blessed Virgin. Never has our hope . . . at any time of our life . . . failed to bear fruit or bring us comfort. Thus encouraged, our hope today rises more confidently than ever to beseech many more and even greater blessings through her favor and mediation." (Leo XIII: Encyclical, *Magnae Dei Matris*, September 8, 1892.)

290. See quotations Nos. 30 and 277 above.

291. "Who can number the secret gifts of grace which God has bestowed upon His Church through the intercession of the Blessed Virgin throughout this period? . . . No sooner had Pius IX proclaimed as a dogma of the Catholic Faith the preservation of Mary from original stain, than the Virgin herself began in Lourdes those wonderful manifestations, followed by the vast and magnificent movements, which have resulted in those two temples dedicated to the Immaculate Mother, where the prodigies which still continue

to take place through her intercession furnish splendid arguments against the incredulity of our days." (St. Pius X: Encyclical, *Ad diem illum*, February 2, 1904.)

292. "John saw the most holy Mother of God already in eternal happiness, yet travailing in a mysterious childbirth. What birth was it? Surely it was the birth of us who, still in exile, are yet to be generated to the perfect charity of God, and to eternal happiness. And the birth pains show the love and desire with which the Virgin from heaven above watches over us, and strives with unwearying prayer to bring about the completion of the elect." (St. Pius X: Encyclical, *Ad diem illum*, February 2, 1904.)

293. "Mother of the Prince of Peace, Mediatrix between rebellious man and the merciful God, she is the dawn of peace shining in the darkness of a world out of joint; she never ceases to implore her Son for peace, although His hour is not yet come; she always intervenes on behalf of sorrowing humanity in the hour of danger; today she who is the Mother of many orphans and our advocate in this tremendous catastrophe will most quickly hear our prayers." (Benedict XV: Allocution, December 24, 1915.)

294. "With your prayers, invoke the kingdom of Christ to which your most beloved Mother urges you with her example, and for which her maternal intercession procures for you all the necessary means; does she not in fact hold a privileged post because of the function which Providence wished to give her in the life of

the Church and in that of each of its members?" (Pius XII: Radio message, September 17, 1958.)

The prayer of Mary, Mediatrix, upholds and substitutes our prayer

295. "If we thus again and again greet Mary, it is precisely that our failing and defective prayers may be strengthened with the necessary confidence; confidence which rises in us thinking that Mary, more than praying for us, prays to God in our name. Nor can our prayers fail to ascend to Him as a sweet savor when commended by the prayers of the Virgin." (Leo XIII: Encyclical, *Jucunda semper*, September 8, 1894.)

Mary intercedes on our behalf

296. "As the sad conditions affecting both the Church and civil society proved to us the extreme need for signal aid from God, it was clear to us that that aid should be sought through the intercession of His Mother." (Leo XIII: Encyclical, *Jucunda semper*, September 8, 1894.)

297. "Trusting in her intercession with Christ Our Lord, who though sole mediator between God and man, wished however to make His Mother the advocate for sinners . . ." (Pius XI: Encyclical, *Miserentissimus Redemptor*, May 8, 1928.)

298. "May the very powerful Mother of God, moved by the prayers of so many of her sons, obtain from her only Son—let us all beseech her—that those who have

miserably wandered from the path of truth and virtue may, with new fervor, find it again." (Pius XII: Encyclical, *Ingruentium malorum*, September 15, 1951.)

299. "Have great trust in the intercession of the most holy Virgin and ask her with all urgency to help you hold fast to your promise." (Pius XII: Allocution, July 17, 1954.)

300. "We deem it advisable to recall that when new dangers threaten the Christian people and the Church, spouse of the divine Saviour, we, as our predecessors have done in past centuries, turn our prayers to the Virgin Mary, most loving mother, and we invite all the faithful entrusted to us to place themselves confidently under her protection." (Pius XII: Encyclical, *Meminisse juvat*, July 14, 1958.)

Mary's intercession is unique

301. "Of all the blessed in heaven, who can compare with the august Mother of God in obtaining grace? Who sees more clearly in the Eternal Word what troubles oppress us, what are our needs? Who is allowed more power in moving God? Who can compare with her in motherly affection? We do not pray to the blessed in the same way as to God: 'for we ask the Holy Trinity to have mercy on us, but we ask all the saints to pray for us.' Yet our manner of praying to the Blessed Virgin has something in common with our worship of God so that the Church even addressed to her the words with which we pray to God: 'Have mercy on sinners.'" (Leo

XIII: Encyclical, *Augustissimae*, September 12, 1897.)

Mary's intercession is most powerful

302. "Mary is all powerful with her divine Son." (Benedict XV: Encyclical, *Fausto appetente die*, June 29, 1921.)

303. "We ardently hope that . . . you will draw from the treasury of the writings and examples of our Saint Louis-Marie de Montfort that which constitutes the basis of his Marian devotion: his firm conviction of the most powerful intercession of Mary." (Pius XII: Allocution, July 21, 1947.)

304. "We have the Virgin as universal advocate in all things, for she is more powerful in whatever necessity than are the other Saints in particular needs." (Pius XII: Radio message, October 12, 1947.)

305. "The 'Fiat' of the Incarnation, her collaboration in the work of her Son, the intensity of the sufferings endured during the passion, and this death of the soul which she experienced on Calvary, had opened the heart of Mary to the universal love of humanity and the decision of her divine Son impressed the seal of omnipotence on her motherhood of grace. Henceforth she consecrated that immense power of intercession with Jesus which her title of Mother confers on her to saving those whom Jesus points out to her from the heights of heaven, saying to her once again, 'Woman, behold thy children.'" (Pius XII: Allocution, July 17, 1954.)

Mary's intercession is assiduous

306. "That most glorious Virgin, exalted above the choirs of the Angels and the countless legions of the Saints, never ceases in heaven to make most efficacious intercession with her Son for all the faithful on earth." (Pius IX: Allocution, December 1, 1854.)

Mary is our advocate

307. "While the prayers of those in heaven have, it is true, some claim on God's watchful eye, the prayers of Mary place their assurance in a mother's right. For that reason, when she approaches her divine Son's throne, as advocate she begs, as handmaid she prays, but as mother she commands." (Pius VII: Apostolic Constitution, *Tanto studo*, February 19, 1805.)

308. "Later, in a complete and permanent way, she will be able to plead our cause when she will have passed into life eternal." (Leo XIII: Encyclical, *Jucunda semper*, September 8, 1894.)

309. "Ah! do thou, our blessed Mother, our queen and advocate . . . gather together our prayers and, we beseech thee (our hearts one with thine), present them before God's throne." (St. Pius X: Prayer composed for the 50th anniversary of the Definition of the Immaculate Conception, September 8, 1903.)

310. "It has been allowed to the august Virgin to be the most powerful mediatrix and advocate of the whole world with her divine Son." (St. Pius X: Encyclical, *Ad diem illum*, February 2, 1904.)

311. "Trusting in her intercession with Christ Our Lord, who though sole mediator between God and man, wished however to make His Mother the advocate for sinners and the dispenser and mediatrix of His grace . . ." (Pius XI: Encyclical, *Miserentissimus Redemptor*, May 8, 1928.)

312. "Though that grace comes from God, it is given through Mary, our advocate and mediatrix . . . We must of necessity wish that the youth of today, exposed as they are to many dangers, should make devotion to Mary the predominant thought of their whole life. By persevering prayer let us make Mary our daily mediatrix, our true advocate. In this way we may hope that she herself, assumed into heavenly glory, will be our advocate before divine goodness and mercy at the hour of our passing." (Pius XI: Allocution, August 15, 1933.)

313. "Conscious of your sufferings, but comforted by the spectacle of your faith that brought you as suppliants to the feet of Mary, Mother of divine love, we have already wanted to be among you to mingle our prayers with yours in one petition. And we were about to carry out our desire to support your confidence in Mary, powerful mediatrix with her divine Son, but the clement Queen and Patron whose kindness not only gives help to Him who asks, but very often freely meets His wish before it is expressed, anticipated our wish." (Pius XII: Allocution to the Faithful of Rome, June 11, 1944.)

314. "With Our Lord may she be blessed whom He constituted Mother of Mercy, queen and our most loving advocate, mediatrix of His graces, dispenser of His treasures." (Pius XII: Radio message, May 13, 1946.)

315. "Our advocate, placed between God and the sinner, takes it upon herself to invoke clemency of the Judge so as to temper His justice, touch the heart of the sinner and overcome His obstinacy." (Pius XII: Allocution, July 21, 1947.)

316. "This is why, O most sweet Mother and most powerful advocate, you wanted to set your spotless foot on that rock of the Pyrenees." (Pius XII: Radio message, September 17, 1958.)

Mary's intercession is universal

317. "Who among all those who are passing through this world, carrying the burden of so many weaknesses and exposed to so many dangers, have no need of assistance? Listen therefore to the Doctor Eximius (Suarez) when he tells you, 'We have the Virgin as universal advocate in all things, for she is more powerful in whatever necessity than are the other Saints in particular needs.'" (Pius XII: Radio message, October 12, 1947.)

PRIVILEGES OF MARY'S PRAYER

Mary is heard because she is Mother, because she is full of grace, because she is united to Christ

318. See quotations Nos. 1, 287 and 306 above.

319. See quotations Nos. 28, 100, 210 and 223 above.

320. "Nor can our prayers fail to ascend to Him as a sweet savor when commended by the prayers of the Virgin. For He, all benign, invites her: 'Let thy voice sound in my ears: for thy voice is sweet.' For this cause do we repeatedly celebrate those glorious titles of her ministry as mediatrix. Her do we greet who found favor with God; who was in a signal manner filled with grace by Him so that the superabundance thereof might overflow upon all men; who was united with the Lord by the most intimate of all bonds; who was blessed among women; and who alone took away the curse and bore the blessing—that Fruit of her womb, that happy Fruit in which all the nations of the earth are blessed. Her do we invoke, finally, as Mother of God, and in virtue of a dignity so sublime, what graces from her may we not promise to ourselves, sinners though we are, in life and in the agonies of death?" (Leo XIII: Encyclical, *Jucunda semper*, September 8, 1894.)

321. "Jesus Christ alone, God and man, is king in the strict, full and absolute sense; but Mary shares in His royal dignity in a secondary way, dependent upon the sovereignty of her Son. She is Mother of the Christ-

God and is His associate in the work of redemption, in His conflict with the enemy and in His complete victory. It is from this union with Christ the King that she receives a height of splendor unequalled in all creation. From this she has her royal power to distribute the treasures of the kingdom of the divine Redeemer. From this union with Christ, her motherly intercession with her Son and with the Father has a power that never fails." (Pius XII: Encyclical, *Ad coeli Reginam*, October 11, 1954.)

Mary's intercession is always efficacious

322. "She obtains all she asks for and her prayer is always heard." (Pius IX: Encyclical: *Exultavit cor nostrum*, November 21, 1851.)

323. "What she asks, she obtains. Her pleas can never be unheard." (Pius IX: Apostolic Constitution, *Ineffabilis Deus*, December 8, 1854.)

324. "The Blessed Virgin, the Mother of God, whose patronage has ever been the most efficacious." (Leo XIII: Encyclical, *Quam pluries*, August 15, 1889.)

325. "Why should not we . . . entrust ourselves and all our interests to her most efficacious intercession? Just as all created things acknowledge and obey the will of God, so may it be stated that Mary's Son ever attends most favorably to the petitions of His Mother." (Pius XII: Letter to Cardinal Maglione, April 15, 1942.)

326. See quotation No. 312 above.

327. See quotation No. 321 above.

328. "In your apostolic labours and the difficulties of your ministry take refuge under her very powerful patronage. If she beseeches her divine Son, you will experience with certainty that there is nothing which you, sustained by divine grace, are unable to bring to a successful issue." (Pius XII: Letter to the Superior General of the Third Order of Carmelites of Malabar, October 30, 1955.)

Mary is in closest contact with God and sees our needs better

329. See quotation No. 301 above.

Mary has the greatest motherly tenderness

330. "Who can compare with her in motherly affection?" (Leo XII: Encyclical, *Augustissimae*, September 12, 1897.)

Mary enjoys the greatest favor of God

331. "He, all benign, invites her: 'Let thy voice sound in my ears: for thy voice is sweet.'" (Leo XII: Encyclical, *Jucunda semper*, September 8, 1894.)

332. "Of all the blessed in heaven, who can compare with the august Mother of God in obtaining grace? . . . For so great is her dignity, so great her favor before God, that whosoever in His need will not have recourse to her is trying to fly without wings." (Leo XIII: Encyclical, *Augustissimae*, September 12, 1897.)

Mary is the person united closest to Christ

333. See quotations Nos. 259, 266 and 321 above.

Mary has rights of possession on the Heart of Jesus

334. See quotation No. 313 above.

Mary brings about the return of warm affection to the hearts of men

335. "Though that grace comes from God, it is given through Mary, our advocate and mediatrix, since motherly affection on the one hand finds response in filial devotion on the other." (Pius XI: Allocution, August 15, 1933.)

This intercession constitutes Mary intercessor of the Omnipotent

336. "That most glorious Virgin who, exalted above the choirs of Angels and the countless legions of the Saints, never ceases in heaven to make most efficacious intercession with her Son for all the faithful on earth." (Pius IX: Allocution, December 1, 1854.)

337. "Now of all the blessed in heaven who can compare with the august Mother of God in obtaining grace? . . . Who is allowed more power in moving God?" (Leo XIII: Encyclical, *Augustissimae*, September 12, 1897.)

338. "The faith of her believers and her children's love consider her not only God's Mother but also

the mediatrix with God." (Benedict XV: Allocution, December 24, 1915.)

339. "How powerful with Jesus must be the intercession of her who was raised to such a high dignity." (Benedict XV: Letter, *Cohaeret plane*, March 21, 1919.)

340. "So powerful, indeed, is the Blessed Virgin with God and His only begotten Son that, as Dante observes, anyone who desires His help and fails to have recourse to Mary is like one trying to fly without wings." (Pius XII: Letter to Cardinal Maglione, April 15, 1940.)

341. See quotation No. 228 above.

THE FRUITS OF MARY'S PRAYER

They appear at Cana

342. "Since the first public miracle performed by our divine Redeemer in Cana of Galilee was brought about by Mary's merciful intercession . . . why should not we . . . entrust ourselves and all our interests to her most efficacious intercession?" (Pius XII: Letter to Cardinal Maglione, April 15, 1942.)

They appear at Pentecost

343. "The example of the Apostles should be borne in mind who, awaiting the supreme gift of the Paraclete promised to them, persevered unanimously in prayer with the Mother of Jesus." (Leo XIII: Encyclical, *Superiore anno*, August 30, 1884.)

344. "You know well the intimate and wonderful relations existing between her and the Holy Spirit, so that she is justly called His spouse. Her intercession was of great avail both in the mystery of the Incarnation and in the coming of the Holy Spirit upon the Apostles." (Leo XIII: Encyclical, *Divinum illud*, May 9, 1897.)

345. "She showed the Apostles at the happy beginning of their priesthood how diligent they should be together in prayer, until they were clothed with virtue from on high; and by the superabundance of her own prayers she surely obtained that virtue for them, at the same time increasing and strengthening it by her counsels, all for the unlimited fruitfulness of their apostolate." (St. Pius X: Exhortation, *Haerent animo*, September 4, 1908.)

346. "May she obtain for you a far-reaching, brotherly and apostolic charity, as she obtained by her prayer in the midst of the first Christians gathered at the Cenacle." (Pius XII: Allocution, July 17, 1954.)

Mary continues to have the Holy Ghost descend on priests

347. "To the beloved Mother of God, mediatrix of heavenly graces, we entrust the priests of the whole world in order that, through her intercession, God will vouchsafe a generous outpouring of His spirit which will move all ministers of the altar to holiness and, through their ministry, will spiritually renew the face

of the earth." (Pius XII: Exhortation, *Menti nostrae*, September 23, 1950.)

Mary showers invisible graces on the Church

348. "Who can number the secret gifts of grace which God has bestowed upon his Church through the intercession of the Blessed Virgin?" (St. Pius X: Encyclical, *Ad diem illum*, February 2, 1904.)

NOTE.—In their official statements the Popes have emphasised in many other ways Our Lady's action in the Church. They tell us that her holiness has a great influence over all the Church, that she takes part in the work fulfilled in the Church by Christ and that she always intercedes for the Church. She never ceases to spend herself for the Church. She is the base, the centre and the link of union between Christians. She enrolls us in the Church and there strives for union in love. As the Seat of Wisdom, she illuminates the Bishops and helps them and renders all people docile to them. As Queen of the Apostolate, she inspires Doctors and promotes the zeal of religious. She procures the dominion and extension of the Church and is its stronghold, help, support, constant refuge, hope and guiding star She watches over the Church, defends it in its dangers and brings to it peace, victory and freedom.

Mary works out our salvation

349. "When we have recourse to Mary in prayer, we are having recourse to the Mother of Mercy, who is so well disposed towards us that, whatever the necessity that presses upon us, especially in attaining eternal life, she is instantly at our side of her own accord, even though she has not been invoked . . . It is a great thing in any Saint to have grace sufficient for the salvation of many souls; but to have enough to suffice for the sal-

vation of everybody in the world is the greatest of all; and this is found in Christ and in the Blessed Virgin." (Leo XIII: Encyclical, *Magnae Dei Matris*, September 8, 1892.)

350. See quotation No. 309 above.

351. "Mary is Mistress of all things because she restores them to their original dignity by the grace which she merited . . . She cooperated in our redemption. She provided her very substance for His body, she offered Him willingly for us, and she took a unique part in our salvation by desiring it, praying for it and so obtaining it." (Pius XII: Encyclical, *Ad coeli Reginam*, October 11, 1954.)

Mary obtains faith for us

352. "In the same holy bosom of His most chaste mother, Christ took to Himself flesh, and united to Himself the spiritual body formed by those who were to believe in Him. Hence Mary, carrying the Saviour within her, may be said to have also carried all those whose life was contained in the life of the Saviour. Therefore all we who are united to Christ, and as the Apostle says, 'are members of His body, of His flesh and of His bones,' have issued from the womb of Mary like a body united to His head. Hence, in a spiritual and mystical fashion, we are all children of Mary, and she is Mother of us all, 'The Mother, spiritually, indeed, but truly the Mother of the members of Christ, whom we

are.' " (St. Pius X: Encyclical, *Ad diem illum*, February 2, 1904.)

353. "Pray to her that she may give you the strength to follow Him to the end with faith." (Pius XII: Allocution, September 29, 1957.)

354. "Through thy powerful intercession, O Mary, may minds and hearts find repose in abandoning themselves to the will of the heavenly Father, in the consciousness of their frailty, in faith in divine promises, in the hope of eternal blessings, and in adhering lovingly to thy crucified Jesus who has made our crosses His own." (Prayer of Pope Pius XII: June 2, 1958.)

Despair disappears with devotion to Mary

355. "Aided by her prayer, they will not despair." (Gregory XVI: Letter to the Archbishop of Prague, April 23, 1845.)

MARY IS THE MEDIATRIX OF OUR PRAYERS

Mary exercises her mediation with regard to our prayers

356. "So that God may more easily hear our prayers and supplications, let us lift our eyes and hands to the Blessed Mother Mary, immaculate Virgin. We could not find a more powerful protectress or one more irresistible before God. She is for us the best of mothers, our safest confidante and in fact the very motive of

our hope: she obtains all she asks for and her prayer is always heard." (Pius IX: Encyclical, *Exultavit cor nostrum*, November 21, 1851.)

357. "All men are filled with the hope and the confidence that the petitions which might be received with less favor from the lips of unworthy men, will be accepted by God when they are recommended by His most holy Mother and will be favorably heard." (Leo XIII: Encyclical, *Octobri mense*, September 22, 1891.)

Mary presents our prayers to God

358. See quotation No. 356 above.

359. "Do thou, our blessed Mother . . . do thou gather together our prayers and we beseech thee (our hearts one with thine) present them before God's throne." (Pius X: Prayer composed for the 50th anniversary of the Definition of the Immaculate Conception, September 8, 1903.)

360. "Full of kindness and love, she transmits to her Son the invocations by which we daily beseech her." (St. Pius X: Allocution to the Franciscans, November 12, 1910.)

Mary stands by our prayers

361. "Nobody knows and comprehends so well as she everything that concerns us: what help we need in life; what dangers, public and private, threaten our welfare; what difficulties and evils surround us; above all, how fierce is the fight we wage with the ruthless ene-

mies of our salvation. In these and in all other troubles of life her power is most far reaching. She has the most ardent desire to bring consolation, strength and help to every race of children so dear to her. Accordingly, let us approach Mary confidently, wholeheartedly, beseeching her by her motherhood which unites her so closely to Jesus and at the same time to us. Let us with deepest devotion invoke her constant aid in the prayer which she herself has indicated and which is most acceptable to her. Then with good reason shall we rest with an easy and a joyful mind under the protection of the best of mothers." (Leo XIII: Encyclical, *Magnae Dei Matris*, September 8, 1892.)

362. "For if we thus again and again greet Mary, it is precisely that our failing and defective prayers may be strengthened with the necessary confidence; confidence which rises in us in thinking that Mary, more than praying for us, prays to God in our name. Nor can our prayers fail to ascend to Him as a sweet savor when commended by the prayers of the Virgin." (Leo XIII: Encyclical, *Jucunda semper*, September 8, 1894.)

363. "St. Germain of Constantinople addresses this prayer to her: 'Be mindful of Christians who are thy servants; commend the prayers of all; help all to realize their hopes; strengthen the faith, keep the Church in unity.'" (Leo XIII: Encyclical, *Adiutricem populi*, September 5, 1895.)

364. "May she continue to strengthen our prayers

with her suffrages." (Leo XIII: Encyclical, *Divinum illud*, May 9, 1897.)

Mary renders our prayers efficacious

365. See quotation No. 357 above.

366. "Let us with one heart entreat and beseech Mary, the Mother of Jesus Christ and our Mother: Show thyself to be a mother; cause our prayers to be accepted by Him who, born for us, consented to be thy Son.'" (Leo XIII: Encyclical, *Octobri mense*, September 22, 1891.)

367. See quotation No. 362 above.

368. "Let all, with humble prayer and entreaty, implore of God, through the intercession of Mary . . . We know, indeed, from experience that such prayer, born of charity and trust in the Virgin, has never been vain." (St. Pius X: Encyclical, *Ad diem illum*, February 2, 1904.)

Mary makes up for the unworthiness of those who pray

369. See quotation No. 358 above.

Mary unites herself to our prayers

370. "We do not doubt that the Virgin Mary, Mother of God and the tender Mother of men, will be favorable to the wishes and prayers that countless crowds of Christians, gathered from every part of the world, will multiply at her shrine, and that she will add

her intercessions to theirs, so that the joint prayerful entreaty will, as it were, do violence to heaven and touch the God of infinite mercy." (Leo XIII: Apostolic Letter, *Parta humano generi*, September 8, 1901.)

THE SECONDARY CONSEQUENCES OF MARY'S MEDIATION

Prayer causes Mary's bounty to, flow on her sons

371. "O Virgin fair as the moon, the delight of heaven, on whose countenance the blessed gaze and the Angels see themselves reflected, make us, thy children, like unto thee, and let our souls receive a ray of thy beauty, which does not fade with the years but shines forth to eternity." (Pius XII: Radio message, December 8, 1953.)

Mary's Mediation makes us grow in the knowledge of God

372. "We are in justice bound to recognise the hidden influence of Mary in obtaining the gift of faith and its salutary cultivation—of Mary who brought the 'Author of Faith' into this world, and who because of her own great faith was called blessed. O Virgin most holy, none abounds in the knowledge of God except through thee; none, O Mother of God, attains salvation except through thee, none receives a gift from the throne of mercy except through thee." (Leo XIII:

Encyclical, *Adiutricem populi*, September 5, 1895.)

373. "It is no exaggeration to say that it is due chiefly to her leadership and help that the wisdom and teachings of the Gospel spread so rapidly to all the nations of the world in spite of the most obstinate difficulties and most cruel persecutions and brought everywhere in their train a new reign of justice and peace. This is what stirred the soul of St. Cyril of Alexandria to the following prayerful address to the Blessed Virgin: 'Through you the Apostles have preached salvation to the nations . . . through you the priceless Cross is everywhere honored and venerated; through you the demons have been put to rout and mankind has been summoned back to heaven; through you every misguided creature held in the thralls of idols is led to recognise the truth; through you have the faithful been brought to the labour of holy baptism and the Church has been founded among every people.' Nay, she has even, as this same Doctor claims, upheld and given strength to the 'scepter of the Orthodox faith.' It has been her unremitting concern to see to it that the Catholic faith stands firmly lodged in the midst of the people, there to thrive in its fertile and undivided unity. Many and well known are the proofs of her solicitude, manifested from time to time even in a miraculous manner." (Leo XIII: Encyclical, *Adiutricem populi*, September 5, 1895.)

374. "Hail, most abundant source from which spring out the streams of divine wisdom, and holds

back, with the purest and clearest sources of orthodoxy, the curling waves of error." (Pius XII: Radio message, October 12, 1945.)

375. "Under the influence and with the help of Mary . . . good thoughts fructify in souls. Perhaps, already at this moment, you are filled with the glory that emanates from the Immaculate Virgin, the Mother of divine grace, the mediatrix of all graces." (Pius XII: Radio message, December 8, 1953.)

376. "When we proclaimed the Marian Year to mark the centenary of the Definition of the Immaculate Conception, we did so precisely with the intention and hope of seeing that living faith, through the powerful intercession of Mary, grow and strengthen itself in the Church." (Pius XII: Radio message, May 16, 1954.)

377. "Be ever to us a Mother, modelling our hearts, enlightening our minds, strengthening our wills, adorning our souls with every virtue, and keeping away from us the enemies of our God who would wish to ruin us for ever." (Pius XII: Prayer, October 28, 1956.)

Mary's Mediation assures holiness

378. "If we consider ever so little how many and powerful are the reasons which prompt this most holy Mother to bestow on us these precious gifts, oh, how our hopes will be expanded. For is not Mary the Mother of Christ? Then she is our Mother also. And we must in truth hold that Christ, the Word made flesh, is also the Saviour of mankind. Now, as the God-man, He had

a material body like that of any other man; and as Saviour of the human family He had a spiritual and mystical body, the society, namely, of those who believe in Christ. So we, being the many, are one body in Christ.' Now the Blessed Virgin did not conceive the eternal Son of God merely that He might be made man, taking His human nature from her, but also in order that by means of the nature assumed from her, He might be the Redeemer of men." (St. Pius X: Encyclical, *Ad diem illum*, February 2, 1904.)

379. "She hastens to show us exiles in this vale of tears, Jesus, the way of salvation." (St. Pius X: Allocution to Franciscans, November 12, 1910.)

380. "If the graces which we receive from the treasury of redemption are distributed, so to speak, by the hands of this sorrowful Virgin, no one can deny that the grace of a happy death must come from Mary because, in fact, it is by means of this pre-eminent grace that the work of redemption reaches its fulfilment in every man. In the same way, the sorrowful Virgin was constituted by Jesus Christ as Mother of all men, and as she received them as a heritage from the infinite love of Jesus, she assumed with motherly love the duty of watching over their spiritual life." (Benedict XV: Letter, *Inter sodalicia*, May 22, 1918.)

381. "'She has been constituted the cause of salvation for the whole human race' (St. Irenaeus)." (Pius XII: Encyclical, *Ingruentium malorum*, September 15, 1951.)

382. "Are you hoping one day to reach Paradise through the grace of perseverance in the last moment of your lives? Are you trusting to die in the grace of God? This grace also will come to you, as those devoted to Mary, through a smile of hers, as a ray from that Sun." (Pius XII: Radio message, December 8, 1953.)

383. "She took a unique part in our salvation by desiring it, praying for it and so obtaining it." (Pius XII: Encyclical, *Ad coeli Reginam*, October 11, 1954.)

Mary builds up the Mystical Body

384. "The Apostle continues, 'and being with child, she cried, travailing in birth, and was in pain to be delivered.' John, therefore, saw the most holy Mother of God, already in eternal happiness yet travailing in a mysterious childbirth. What birth was it? Surely it was the birth of us who, still in exile, are yet to be generated to the perfect charity of God, and to eternal happiness. And the birth pains show the love and desire with which the Virgin from heaven also watches over us, and strives with unwearying prayer to bring about the completion of the number of the elect." (St. Pius X: Encyclical, *Ad diem illum*, February 2, 1904.)

385. "Upon the mystical Body of Christ, born of the broken Heart of the Saviour, she bestowed that same motherly care and fervent love with which she fostered and nurtured the suckling Infant Jesus in the cradle." (Pius XII: Encyclical, *Mystici Corporis*, June 29, 1943.)

See also quotation No. 352.

The Popes go on to tell us that through her mediation, Mary grants peace and pleases God, opens heaven, puts the devil to flight and obtains victory over present enemies.